MANAGING HUMAN RESOURCES IN THE PUBLIC SECTOR

A Shared Responsibility

MANAGING HUMAN RESOURCES IN THE PUBLIC SECTOR

A Shared Responsibility

GILL ROBINSON HICKMAN
and
DALTON S. LEE

FOREWORD BY N. JOSEPH CAYER

HARCOURT COLLEGE PUBLISHERS

Fort Worth   Philadelphia   San Diego   New York   Orlando   Austin   San Antonio
Toronto   Montreal   London   Sydney   Tokyo

PUBLISHER   Earl McPeek
EXECUTIVE EDITOR   David Tatom
MARKET STRATEGIST   Laura Brennan
PROJECT MANAGER   Barrett Lackey

ISBN: 0-15-507384-2
Library of Congress Catalog Card Number: 00-106353

Address for Domestic Orders
Harcourt College Publishers, 6277 Sea Harbor Drive, Orlando, FL 32887-6777
800-782-4479

Address for International Orders
International Customer Service
Harcourt College Publishers, 6277 Sea Harbor Drive, Orlando, FL 32887-6777
407-345-3800
(fax) 407-345-4060
(e-mail) hbintl@harcourtbrace.com

Address for Editorial Correspondence
Harcourt College Publishers, 301 Commerce Street, Suite 3700,
Fort Worth, TX 76102

Web Site Address
http://www.harcourtcollege.com

Printed in the United States of America

0 1 2 3 4 5 6 7 8 9   039   9 8 7 6 5 4 3 2 1

Harcourt College Publishers

To my family
Michael, Kimberly, Michael B.,
Stephen, Ryan, and my mother,
Beatrice Price

To my wife Laura and our late
friend, Sharon, whose strength
and courage we deeply admired

———————■———————

CONTENTS

FOREWORD

Managing human resources challenges public administrators and agencies because employees are the critical resource in getting the work done. Traditionally, top-level management perceived human resources management as a staff function to be conducted by the personnel department (now the human resources department). Epitomized by the underlying assumptions of the Civil Service Reform Act of 1978, human resources now is considered a central, integrated part of management. As such, traditional personnel departments have been transformed into human resources departments in many jurisdictions and their roles have changed. The role has shifted to one of support for management rather than one of policing managers, supervisors, and employees. While monitoring remains an element of the human resources function, the emphasis now is on serving the needs of the operating departments through assistance and consultation.

Hickman and Lee use the changing role of human resources as one of the foundations for their approach to managing human resources. More importantly, they recognize that human resources management responsibility rests on managers and supervisors throughout the organization. While most other public personnel or human resources management books pay lip service to the role of all managers and supervisors in managing human resources, they rarely actually operationalize it in their examination of the subject. As emphasized by the title, *Managing Human Resources in the Public Sector: A Shared Responsibility* carries through on the promise to treat human resources management as a responsibility of all managers and supervisors in the public organization. They also observe that employees share in some of the responsibility.

The authors integrate discussion of the changing nature of work organizations and their implications for human resources. In doing so, they consider how the organization can be most effective in managing personnel. They also recognize that the reality of the workplace is that the front-line supervisors and managers have the most constant and direct contact with the people who do the work. The supervisors and managers need understanding of human resource issues and the tools to assure the effective working of the organization. Throughout the book, the authors consistently explain the role of the operating departments/units and the human resources units. Thus, readers see clearly how the responsibilities are shared. It becomes very clear that managing human resources requires a lot of skill and cooperation between the operating unit and the human resources unit.

The book covers human resources management thoroughly. Every aspect of human resources receives detailed attention and the separate and common responsibilities of all the responsible parties are considered. To facilitate understanding, tables and figures present material very effectively. The authors capture the essence of their presentations through interesting and attractive displays. They also use exercises to provide an opportunity for readers to apply and test their understanding of the material. Hickman and Lee employ an innovative approach in their exercises. In each chapter, they include exercises for in-service and pre-service students. Clearly, they understand the dynamics of most classes in public human resources management where there is a mix of students with little or no work experience and those who have some or a lot of experience. In order to make exercises useful to those with different levels of experience, these different types of exercises are very effective. They allow students to participate regardless of their backgrounds. The workshop format of the exercises provides an opportunity for students to make presentations in addition to examining and deciding upon application of the material they have learned.

Hickman and Lee have captured the material in a very easy-to-read, engaging writing style. They integrate very effective examples into the discussion of every topic. The reader easily makes the transition from an interesting story to the illustration of an important point about human resources management. The language is clear, to the point, and thought provoking. The reader is left with a good understanding of the elements of human resources management and with a sense of what are good practices as well as a framework for analyzing situations in the workplace.

The authors also include some topics that usually are not found in human resources books. For example, they include an examination and suggestion for "Organizational Assistance Plans." Such plans emulate Employee Assistance Plans, but focus on what issues affect the organization's ability to accomplish its goals. While others have focused on organizational assessment and organization development, these authors integrate such discussions with the day-to-day practice of human resources management activities. The discussion demonstrates the creative way in which the authors examine and present their ideas. They also include a chapter on employee safety and health, giving those topics their appropriate status in discussion of human resources management issues.

In a fitting conclusion to their discussion, Hickman and Lee examine human resources for the new millennium. Their analysis of the forces of change and their impact on human resources management goes far beyond the usual token statement of trends and suggestions for how organizations and managers should consider them. They provide in-depth analysis of the trends and real-life impact of them in public organizations. They wrap it all up with discussion of the Person-Centered Management approach, which was conceptualized by Hickman in the 1980s. The approach integrates the types of concerns all managers should have in managing their organizations. It conceives of management as having to deal with people in their organizations as complex beings who cannot separate their lives into work and non-work segments. Instead, managing human beings requires being sensitive to the many facets of the individual and their effects for the workplace. Person-Centered Management focuses on five components: management roles, employee responsibilities, mutual expectations of managers and employees, personal expectations, and human resource managers' responsibilities. These five components address the concerns of contemporary public management. The authors have captured the essence of modern management theory in their presentation of Person-Centered Management.

This book gives the reader a realistic view of human resources management in public organizations and does so in straightforward prose. Anyone who works in public organizations or studies them will profit from reading *Managing Human Resources in the Public Sector: A Shared Responsibility.*

N. Joseph Cayer
Mesa, Arizona

PREFACE

Department managers in the public sector share responsibility with the human resource department to assure that human resource procedures and practices are carried out with the utmost care and attention. In view of this shared responsibility, it is vital for each side to understand its role in relation to the other. Many texts in the field explain human resource management primarily from the perspective of the human resource department. However, a considerable number of individuals who take courses and workshops on this topic intend to use the information in their roles as department managers or supervisors rather than as human resource administrators. Accordingly, this book describes and illustrates the department manager's role more explicitly in the human resource process. It also provides enough background and history about human resource management in the public sector for department managers to appreciate why the field functions as it does.

For current human resource managers, or those individuals who aspire to become human resource managers, the focus of this book is significant because it emphasizes the mutuality of your role and responsibilities *in conjunction with* those of the department manager. Human resource managers must depend on department managers to implement numerous aspects of the human resource function effectively on a day-to-day basis. The human resource department's function becomes considerably more difficult, if not impossible, when department managers feel alienated from the process or do not understand the purpose and importance of human resource policies, procedures, and accompanying laws.

Based on this premise, we attempt to provide a balance in each chapter between contributing to the reader's understanding of major concepts in human resource management and providing the information needed by aspiring department and human resource managers. Chapter 1, "Understanding Human Resource Management and the Department Manager's Role," outlines the department and human resource managers' involvement in the human resource function and provides a brief historical context for understanding the field. Chapter 2, "Staffing the Department," focuses on the role of the human resource department and department manager in recruitment, testing, and selection. Chapter 3, "Position Management: Understanding the Employee's Job," describes the respective roles of the human resource and department managers in dealing with job analysis, position descriptions, classification, compensation, and merit pay. Chapter 4, "Meeting Departmental Goals: Performance Assessment," evaluates the issues and problems involved in performance appraisal and describes several contemporary approaches. Chapter 5, "Managing Performance Improvement," concentrates on the human resource and department managers' roles in performance counseling, traditional and positive discipline, and due process. Chapter 6, "Employee Safety and Health," discusses maintaining a safe work environment, dealing with enforcement issues concerning health and safety regulations, and working with injured employees. Chapter 7, "Workplace Ethics," examines issues concerning ethical behavior and decision making in the workplace. Finally, Chapter 8, "The New Millennium Workplace," describes the changing demographics and employee expectations in the twenty-first century and a process for meeting these challenges called Person-Centered Management (PCM).

ACKNOWLEDGMENTS

The authors wish to thank the many individuals who supported us on the journey to make this project a reality. Gill Robinson Hickman would like to thank her husband, Michael Hickman, who provided his loving support, time, talent, research assistance, and expertise in human resource management to help complete this book. A major debt of gratitude goes to Joe Cayer and Shirley Williams for reading drafts, contributing their expertise, and most of all providing their sustained friendship and encouragement to keep going despite numerous delays and obstacles. Without Michael, Joe, and Shirley, this book would never have been completed. Special recognition and acknowledgment go to many former M.P.A. students at California State University, Dominguez Hills for providing the inspiration for this book and contributing valuable input and critique concerning its content. Many thanks go to Judy Mable who created the charts for the book and completed much of the word processing for the manuscript. Special appreciation goes to Angie Mims and Amy Keown for their research, technical editing, perfectionism, good cheer, and help in getting me to the finish line. Finally, a huge debt of gratitude goes to Dorothy Dixon who took such loving care of Ryan through long hours and many days and evenings to allow the completion of this and several other major projects.

Dalton Lee thanks his wife, Laura, for her loving patience during the completion of yet another project in this academic saga, which we have shared. A special thanks also to Joe Cayer, who encouraged me to enter the halls of academe and has been a steadfast friend and mentor these many years. Finally, to the many hundreds of students whom it has been a pleasure to meet, thank you for having shared your stories of both hope and struggle. Ultimately, it is your success over adversity that validates what we do.

MANAGING HUMAN RESOURCES IN THE PUBLIC SECTOR

A Shared Responsibility

UNDERSTANDING HUMAN RESOURCE MANAGEMENT AND THE DEPARTMENT MANAGER'S ROLE

INTRODUCTION

What do police chiefs, parks and recreation directors, social services administrators, and information systems directors have in common? Despite vast differences in the goals of their organizational units, they are all responsible for managing the same human resource functions at the departmental level—selection of employees, appraisal of performance, establishment of work standards, improvement of performance, resolution of grievances, promotion of diversity initiatives, compliance with equal employment opportunity and affirmative action, and implementation of health and safety standards. These functions are frequently viewed as the duty solely of the human resource department, but should be considered a shared responsibility between human resource and department managers. Since human resource management is considered a staff function, it must depend on department managers to effectively implement the content of many of the programs, policies, and guidelines under the purview of the human resource department.[1] Human resource administrators do not have line authority and therefore cannot compel department managers to comply with human resource policies. This does not mean, however, that managers can do what they want when it comes to human resource practices.

Many lawsuits have been filed and millions of dollars lost due to inadequate knowledge of human resource practices at the department manager level. Therefore, it is essential that department managers in the public sector understand their role and their responsibilities in this vital area. In certain circumstances such as sexual harassment lawsuits, the failure of a department manager to keep informed (as well as a failure to inform subordinates of their obligation not to engage in harassment) can have unfavorable consequences for the organization and the individual manager. Not only is ignorance of the applicable policies no defense, but managers who use it as a defense may find themselves personally liable. Since lack of knowledge only demonstrates malfeasance of office, dereliction of duty, and willful disregard of directives, the organization will likely conclude that it is not obligated to defend the accused manager.

UNDERSTANDING THE
HUMAN RESOURCE DEPARTMENT

According to department managers, the human resource department often frustrates their efforts with excuses about rules and regulations. Replacing an employee who has resigned ought to be done quickly, but all too often takes months to accomplish. Managers' frustrations are understandable, but that is only part of the story. Human resource departments in the public sector are obliged, first of all, to conform to the laws, and they must carefully weave their way through the federal, state, and local regulations that may apply. Fulfilling legal requirements is always a challenge, and it frequently takes more time than managers would like. But the failure to comply can have serious consequences. When replacing an employee, for example, a failure to comply with applicable laws may lead to the filing of grievances or a lawsuit. The result will be considerable expenditures of time and resources and the involvement of government agencies with oversight, investigative, and enforcement powers. In short, more time and money will be spent than would otherwise be the case. The fact that human resource requirements in the public sector are not simple should come as no great surprise. A brief look at the historical background will provide insight into the origin and purpose of these requirements.

BRIEF HISTORICAL OVERVIEW

Human resource management (previously known as public personnel administration) can be traced back to key social and political events. When our first president, George Washington, took office, his selection of staff on the basis of good character, education, and loyalty to the newly formed United States of America was clearly a reaction to the nepotism and cronyism of English colonialism. Because Washington's human resource practices were a significant statement about the way in which government should be run, it is not surprising that many of them are still with us today in the form of reference and background checks and education requirements for employment. Washington thought it necessary to staff his administration with representatives from each of the newly formed United States and, more important, to have the explicit approval of the applicable state senators because of the shortcomings and eventual failure of the loosely configured confederation of states. Although unique in its time, this human resource practice has become so commonplace today for high-level appointments that we almost take senatorial confirmation for granted.

Most of the practices found in today's human resource departments can be traced back to the 1800s. To a large degree, these human resource practices were reactions to the social and political events of the time. Newly

enfranchised voters from the former Western territories swept President Andrew Jackson into office. Jackson ran for the presidency promising that he
would put entrenched, elitist bureaucrats out of office and replace them with
ordinary people who would be responsive to his new policies and political
agenda. Although he was not the first, Jackson popularized a system of rotation in office that rewarded political supporters and democratized the public
service by making government jobs available to the average American. He felt
that a system of political patronage, appointment to government positions
based primarily on political party loyalty, would make government workers
more responsive to the administration. In order to provide broader access to
these positions, jobs could be rotated to provide government positions to more
people as a reward for their political allegiance. Ironically, Jackson did not
create substantial turnover during his tenure. An unintended consequence of
his human resource practices was to open the door for massive dismissals
that disrupted the work of government and led to charges of political corruption and ineptness in subsequent administrations. This process of rotation in
office ultimately became known as the "spoils system" as each new political
incumbent distributed the spoils of victory to the party faithful. Since new
employees were picked primarily on the basis of their political loyalty rather
than their ability to do the job, the patronage system was open to accusations
of corruption. There were those who worried that favoritism and self-interest
might replace the public interest, and there were those who advocated a neutral professionalism as the proper ethic of government employees.

Surprisingly, the most corrupt federal administration may have been the
one under the leadership of a man we have all come to revere, President Abraham Lincoln. There is considerable evidence to show that contracts for war
matériel and supplies during the Civil War were given to political cronies
who profiteered while leaving Union soldiers with shoes that fell apart, cloth-
ing that exposed them to the elements, food that was made from rotten meat,
and munitions that did more harm to the user than the intended target.

When General Ulysses S. Grant became president, he tried to improve human resource practices by creating a Civil Service Commission to ensure that
only the best qualified were hired for government work. He was motivated
both by what he had experienced during the Civil War and by his own personal experience at having lost a county engineer job in Missouri solely because he did not have the necessary political sponsorship. Grant's 1871 Civil
Service Commission approved new human resource practices such as competitive civil service examinations and the "rule of three." The idea that the
appointing authority must pick from only those candidates receiving the top
three scores is a human resource practice that is still with us.[2] Unfortunately,
Grant's Civil Service Commission was short-lived due to lack of congres-
sional funding.

After the assassination of President James Garfield by Charles Guiteau, a
disgruntled party member who did not get a patronage appointment, civil
service reformers and prominent newspaper editors who were fed up with

government corruption successfully pushed for the passage of the Pendleton Act of 1883. This law ended the spoils system and initiated a civil service system which established a merit-based approach to the appointment and advancement of regular government workers.[3] No longer would political loyalty be valued more highly than the ability to do the job. Only those who could demonstrate merit—the qualifications to do the work—would be considered for regular government jobs. The original components of the law are still with us today and focus on three basic tenets: selection based on merit and competitive testing; protection from dismissal for political reasons; and protection for government workers against required participation in political activities. After the enactment of the Pendleton Act by the federal government, many state and local governments also adopted merit-based civil service systems. Not until the passage of the Social Security Act in the late 1930s, however, did Congress require all states to have a civil service system based on merit.[4]

Because many of our ideas about the civil service system were formed as a reaction to the spoils system, a major focus of modern-day human resource practices became the prevention of unwanted political activities. Thus, many of the ensuing rules and regulations found in human resource departments were not designed to enable managerial actions but were enacted to prevent the abuses that the spoils system created.

Current human resource practices make a positive contribution to the workplace even though they were formed out of a reaction to political excesses of the past. The constructive component of this system focuses on providing open access and competition. Historically, the "open competition" component of the merit system included the following:

1. *Adequate publicity.* Job openings and requirements must be made public so that interested citizens have a reasonable opportunity to know about them.

2. *Opportunity to apply.* Citizens who are interested must have a chance to make their interest known and to receive consideration.

3. *Realistic standards.* Qualification standards must be reasonably related to the job to be filled and must be applied impartially to all who make their interest known.

4. *Absence of discrimination.* The standards used must contain factors that are related only to ability and fitness for employment.

5. *Ranking on the basis of ability.* The very essence of competition implies a ranking of candidates on the basis of a relative evaluation of their ability and fitness, and a selection process which gives effect to this ranking.

6. *Knowledge of results.* The public must be able to find out how the process works, and anyone who believes that the process has not been applied properly in his or her own case must have a chance for administrative review.[5]

Today, these merit components are an inherent part of human resource practices in the public sector. It takes time to ensure that the best applicants are sought and the most-qualified candidate is selected. Even with a minimal announcement time of two weeks, the process still requires two weeks or more to review the applications, set up a competitive examination process, score the results, and certify the eligible candidates, and at least two weeks between the time the candidate is offered the job and appears for work. Two to three months may have passed before a vacant position is filled. Though most managers would agree that these are professionally sound policies for recruitment and selection, managers are often frustrated by the time lag required by the human resource department. Sooner rather than later the anxious manager needs someone to do the work that does not stop while a candidate is being selected.

EXTERNAL REGULATIONS

There are numerous external laws, regulations, and guidelines that must be incorporated into internal procedures used by the human resource department. These outside regulations affect every function in the human resource department. They ensure that fairness and true merit are the bases for human resource actions. These external factors include collective bargaining laws, equal employment and affirmative action regulations, occupational health and safety regulations, and discipline and due process requirements. Various aspects of these external factors will be discussed in subsequent chapters.

Due to these factors, a simple request submitted to the human resource department by a public sector manager usually requires attention to numerous details of which the department manager may not be aware. Managers often ask why the human resource department cannot be more flexible by modifying, bending, or even suspending some of the regulations to help facilitate their urgent needs. Even the most service-oriented human resource professionals know all too well the organizational consequences of noncompliance. The bottom line equals lawsuits, extensive monetary damages, and hours of staff time spent in responding to compliance agencies and appearing before arbitrators or judges.

CHANGING TIMES

In the past a bipartisan civil service commission governed the typical human resource department. Because the civil service system grew out of concerns that each political party would hire and promote only its own, members of the civil service commission were appointed from each political party. Therefore, opposing viewpoints were represented, and no particular party had an advantage. The temptation by the political party in office to approve human resource policies favorable to itself was moderated by the realization that those same policies might benefit another political party when it came to power. Though a number of state and local governments still use civil service commissions, civil service reform continues to change the structure, functions, and reporting relationship of public human resource systems.

Contemporary civil service reform is not as reactionary as past civil service reform; nonetheless, it continues to refine the principles of a merit system. For example, the federal government has continued to improve the civil service system since the passage of the Civil Service Reform Act of 1978, and recent programs such as "reinventing government" have also had notable effects. A number of state and local governments have abolished their civil service systems and moved to human resource systems that report to the organization's chief administrator. This latter approach allows the human resource department to serve as direct support to top administrators and the human resource director to participate as an integral member of the management team. Even in some organizations with civil service commissions, the structure has been modified to allow an internal management team approach. These kinds of human resource offices function as inside participants rather than outside regulators and are intended to be more responsive to the overall needs of administrators and managers in the organization.

One reason why this type of change can exist without necessarily resurrecting the spoils system is that merit principles and practices, with their emphasis on testing, competition, and ability, have been incorporated over the years into the procedures and processes of the organization. Another reason is that past inclusion of Equal Employment Opportunity (EEO) and Affirmative Action (AA) laws and regulations reinforce many of the open-competition principles and practices normally protected by civil service systems, such as adequate publicity, opportunity to apply, and realistic qualification standards. Stronger merit practices still remain in the area of open competition even though AA laws are being overturned in some states and decreased by Supreme Court decisions. In addition, career managers and professionals with expertise in public administration rather than political appointees are increasingly running government organizations. The complexity of today's public policy issues and the managerial means needed to implement these policies effectively and efficiently require technical knowledge and specialization unfamiliar to the typical party loyalist. Finally, case law increasingly supports human resource policy and practices that are consistent with merit principles.

These contemporary civil service reforms have helped provide opportunities for public human resource departments to become more management oriented, but they have not eliminated the complexities, the time lines, and the regulations required of these offices. Even in large private sector companies, human resource departments resemble their public sector counterparts to a great extent due to such factors as collective bargaining agreements, wrongful discharge case law, and occupational health and safety regulations.

FACILITATING A SERVICE ORIENTATION

Despite the complex factors described above, human resource departments are expected to be service oriented and can serve that function in several ways:

- providing informational sessions for users/clients (i.e., executive managers, department heads, and employees) concerning how various functions and processes actually work within the human resource department, helping to demystify the operation;
- searching for flexible alternatives within the human resource system to assist department managers with their human resource needs;
- seeking input systematically from internal users/clients of the human resource department concerning needed improvements; and
- proposing changes in policies, procedures, or practices that will provide better responsiveness to department, employee, and organizational needs.

An obvious yet important factor in this process is the responsibility of the human resource department to maintain integrity in the implementation of its functions and services. In attempting to provide a service orientation to the organization, human resource managers must walk a fine line between being flexible and maintaining fair standards, so that their practices do not become suspect or compromised within the organization.

THE DEPARTMENT MANAGER'S ROLE

The department manager also has a major role in assisting the human resource department in the implementation of its services and functions. The manager should

- attend workshops and training sessions concerning human resource functions and policies and request that supervisors attend;
- review and follow the human resource policies and procedures governing such functions as recruitment, selection, affirmative action, performance appraisal, employee discipline, and classification (these policies are typically found in human resource handbooks and collective bargaining contracts);
- make these policies and procedures available to supervisors in his/her unit;
- request specialized or tailored sessions on human resource issues for the department when necessary;
- contact the human resource department when there is confusion or uncertainty about policies and procedures; and

■ discuss problems and need for change with the human resource department to facilitate better service and understanding between line departments and human resources.

Understanding Human Resource Management and the Department Manager's Role

PRE-SERVICE STUDENTS

Who's in Charge Here?

The purpose of this discussion is to explore how department managers and personnel specialists can work together better.

Instructions:

■ Divide the class in half: one group will represent department managers and the other group will represent human resource administrators.

■ Have each group read the scenario, then prepare and present an argument for their side. (The instructor may provide additional information about local personnel practices.)

■ How can each side get the other to understand its perspective? Discuss the ways in which both sides can work together to attain a reasonable solution.

Scenario:

The Situation: In early January, the department secretary retired. Needing someone to do the job and knowing that it would take a while for the position to be filed, the department manager, Ms. Jacobs, felt she had little choice but to hire an interim secretary. Interim staff can be temporarily hired into a vacant position for up to ninety days, but have no guarantee that they will be hired permanently. They must compete for the position in order to be hired permanently. Ms. Jacobs is happy with the work of the interim temporary secretary and hopes that she will have an opportunity to hire her from the eligibility list. In mid-February, she calls the Human Resource Department (HRD) to find out when she can expect a copy of the eligibility list. HRD tells her that the list will not be certified before April because the original list had expired in early February. The position then had to be advertised, applications taken, interviews conducted, and offers made.

Manager's Concerns: The interim temp had told Ms. Jacobs that her name was on the eligibility list for secretaries (now expired) and that if she was not hired she was going to look elsewhere. As a result of the delay, Ms. Jacobs will lose a good interim employee before the hiring process can be completed and, as a result, have to spend a lot of time training a new employee. Meanwhile, work will go undone or be shifted to other staff employees who are already overworked. If Ms. Jacobs assigns the work to other employees, her overworked staff may follow through on their threat to quit or stage a "sick-out."

HRD's Concerns: Eligibility lists are regularly certified for limited periods of time (e.g., six months to one year). The eligibility list for the position of secretary was over a year old when it was retired. Most of the candidates remaining on the list were already passed over by other departments and were probably not the best candidates available. The merit system requires recruiting and selecting the best candidate. It takes time to publicize the position, collect and screen applications, interview candidates, and put together an eligibility list in accordance with merit policies and practices.

Patronage or Merit?

The objective of this exercise is to gain insight into the debate over patronage and merit.

Instructions:

- Divide the class into teams.
- Each team will be assigned the same task but conduct their research using different resources, such as

  - the Internet
  - periodicals/journals on personnel, public administration, political science, management
  - books in the library
  - interviews with personnel managers
  - interviews with politicians
  - interviews with members of a civil service commission

The Task:

Where is *patronage* most prevalent today? Who benefits from patronage? What are the advantages and disadvantages of patronage? Is a *merit system* appropriate for contemporary public sector organizations? Provide information to support your response. What are the recent trends in merit system reform and why are these trends significant?

IN-SERVICE STUDENTS

Instructions:

Form groups of approximately five members with at least one supervisor or manager from the class included in each group. If there are no supervisors or managers in the class, have each group arrange to bring one or more public sector managers to class for the workshop or interview prior to the session concerning the workshop project described below.

Workshop Project

Ask line or department managers to describe their perceptions of the service provided by the human resource department to their organization. Ask them to provide specific reasons for their perceptions (positive or negative). If there are negative perceptions, ask the managers and class members to suggest ways to improve services, processes, or procedures to help facilitate departmental human resource needs while remaining within the purview of external laws and requirements. If there are positive perceptions, ask managers to describe these programs, services, and/or relationships. Determine how department managers normally pursue having their recommendations addressed in their organization. How should the human resource department, department managers, and other executive managers be involved in the resolution of issues involving the functioning and service of the human resource department with other departments in the agency?

If the perceptions are positive, determine what the human resource department is doing well from the perspective of the department managers. Determine how the human resource department, department managers, and other executive managers work together in these organizations to resolve or address the functioning and service of the human resource department.

Determine whether the managers involved in the workshop perceive the human resource department as a member of the management team of their organization. Why or why not? Do they perceive this as positive or negative? Why or why not?

To enhance the workshop discussion, students or the instructor can invite or interview human resource managers to provide the human resource department's perspective on the issues outlined above.

NOTES

1. Human resource manager or administrator and personnel manager or director are used interchangeably throughout the book. Department manager and line manager are also used interchangeably, as well as human resource manager, human resource specialist, human resource professional, and personnel specialist.

2. In some jurisdictions, there may be a rule of five or seven—that is, those with the top five or seven scores must be interviewed.

3. The civil service system does not cover political appointees, such as undersecretaries, who serve at the pleasure of the executive.

4. U.S. Office of Personnel Management, "1938 Advisory Council Report—The Social Security Board's Comments and Recommendations" in Office of Personnel Management [database online] (Washington, D.C.: Office of Personnel Management [cited 20 June 2000]), available from http://www.opm.gov.

5. O. Glenn Stahl, *Public Personnel Administration* (New York: Harper and Row, 1983), 36.

2

STAFFING THE DEPARTMENT

Each position in the department is vital and designed to contribute to the goals of the unit and organization. Filling these positions with people who have the desire, capacity, and ability to do the job will determine how quickly and effectively these goals are accomplished. Staffing, therefore, is one of the most critical functions in the organization. Department and human resource managers form an interdependent team in this process of attracting and hiring the best employees.

The staffing function involves recruitment, testing, and selection. Many hours and dollars are spent preparing and placing recruitment ads, developing tests, participating in screening and interview processes, and orienting and training new employees. The consequences of error in the process are high in both human and fiscal resources. Picking a person who turns out to be unable to do the work is frustrating for managers, workers, and human resource specialists as well as for the person who was selected. Productivity suffers, time is wasted, and frustration mounts as workers pick up the slack for the incompetent employee. In time, the position becomes vacant and the hiring process must begin all over again.

By the same token, systematically excluding qualified candidates can also be expensive. Not only does the organization miss the opportunity to utilize these candidates' talents, but charges of discrimination may trigger legal action. An external review by federal and state regulators could result in significant sanctions and expensive, time-consuming lawsuits.

THE IMPACT OF AFFIRMATIVE ACTION AND DIVERSITY ON THE STAFFING PROCESS

Affirmative action is under tremendous attack in today's environment. California, a state with one of the most diverse populations in the country, passed the controversial law Proposition 209 "that eliminates race and sex as factors in a variety of state programs, from hiring to education and contracting."[1] On November 3, 1998, 58 percent of Washington voters passed the comparable Initiative 200.[2] These laws effectively end affirmative action in government agencies and public education in the state. What does this mean for public sector organizations in the rest of the country? As indicated by human resource expert Norma Riccucci,

> The legal status of EEO and affirmative action will continue to erode as we move into the twenty-first century. Moreover, Congress and the president, because of attitudes and beliefs of a large segment of the American populace, can no longer offer unconditional support for affirmative action. In light of these phenomena, human resourceists, human resource specialists, and researchers are turning their attention toward workplace diversification endeavors . . .[3]

In addition to the passage of Proposition 209 in California and Initiative 200, other states such as Texas, Louisiana, and Mississippi have adopted similar measures with regard to college admission.[4] Riccucci concludes that some government employers will voluntarily develop and maintain diversity programs despite voter initiatives to end mandated affirmative action programs.[5] In fact, this trend has already begun among state universities and other organizations that have not been able to recruit adequate numbers of minorities and women since the elimination of AA laws in their states. Affirmative action is still the law in the federal government and in states where it has not been eliminated legally—but for how long? The answer will depend on the outcome of events in the states where AA has been eliminated and the desire of the voting public in other states. In the meantime, affirmative action requires employers to take positive action to ensure that persons in protected classes (women, minorities, persons with disabilities, and others) are represented equitably in the organization.

The term "affirmative action" tends to be misunderstood and often interpreted as exclusionary or quota-driven, even though federal and state regulations, executive orders, and laws do not contain the provisions that many people believe exist. Thus, "diversity" is the term being embraced currently by employers to build an inclusive work place. Diversity, rather than affirmative action, has become identified with a more comprehensive view of participants in the workforce. Issues of diversity tend to focus on protected classes—minorities or the disabled, and in more recent years homosexuals have received increasing attention. Still, diversity indicates more subtle differences as well:

> [D]iversity can also include differences in underlying attributes or non-observable differences, such as working styles, values, and personality types, as well as differences in culture, socioeconomic background or professional orientation, industry experience, organizational membership, and group tenure.[6]

The concept of diversity has been more widely supported due to its emphasis on inclusiveness, especially with regard to its incorporation of white males into the complex mix of human resource issues. Many practices and legal decisions that occurred during the implementation of affirmative action left white males feeling alienated and disenfranchised in recruitment, selection, and promotion processes.

Cities such as Santa Ana and San Diego in California and Seattle, Washington, have launched successful diversity programs. These and other effective diversity programs have several key elements in common according to Chambers and Riccucci:

- on-going training and education;
- strong leadership;
- resource commitment;
- recognition of the business necessities of a diverse work force— remaining competitive, developing the ability to hire quality workers and improving the effectiveness of service delivery;
- holding managers accountable; and
- a view of diversity as a way of life and an inherent component of the culture, not just a method for increasing the representation of women and people of color.[7]

Though diversity implies differences, organizations are becoming oriented to the concept of differences as "value-added" resources.[8] This is particularly important as organizational structures become reorganized into teams and the multiple perspectives of team members add strength to the final decisions and outcomes. Diverse teams that work effectively function interdependently and maximize the strengths of the whole while working toward a common goal or purpose.[9] Like our democracy, which gains its strength from the participation of all citizens, today's leaders achieve more creative, productive, and satisfactory outcomes when there is widespread input. The role of department and human resource managers is to prepare, train, and coach the workforce to enhance the diversity and interdependence that contribute to successful collaboration in today's organizations.

AN OVERVIEW OF THE STAFFING PROCESS

How do managers select the right person for the job? Finding an appropriate match between the person, the task, and the work team requires that the manager and human resource department use multiple selection techniques. Job-related selection techniques are the most technically and legally reliable tools to help managers obtain the right person for a particular position; however, human resource professionals will readily admit that the current methods available in the field are sound but not guaranteed to produce total success.

The staffing process requires multiple steps and a considerable period of time due to the inherent requirements of merit systems and the many legal requirements. Table 2-1 illustrates a typical staffing process in public sector organizations. The department and human resource managers are responsible for completing the steps in the staffing process and serve as the primary

TABLE 2-1 STEPS IN A TYPICAL STAFFING PROCESS

Function	Department Manager's Responsibility	Human Resource Manager's Responsibility
Recruitment		P
■ Minimum qualifications		P
■ Specialized qualifications	S	P
Testing		
a. Application/Résumé Screening		P
b. Written Tests	S	P
c. Performance Tests	S	P
d. Qualifying Interview	S	P
Formation of List of Eligible Candidates		P
Certification of Top Candidate(s) to Department Manager		P
Selection Interview	P	
Selection of Final Candidate	P	
Reference Check	S	P
Preemployment Medical Assessment (if applicable)		P
Formal Appointment of Candidate		P
Supervision of Probationary Period		
a. Orientation and training	P (Departmental)	P (HR formal training)
b. Placement and assignment	P	
c. Evaluation	P	S

P = Primary responsibility; S = Secondary participation or responsibility in some organizations. The steps in this table may not apply to every public sector organization. The content of the table is based on the experience of the authors as human resource practitioners, department managers, and subject matter experts.

or secondary participant and evaluator. Each step in the process is detailed throughout the remainder of the chapter.

RECRUITMENT

Although department managers normally do not play an overt role in the recruitment process, they can contribute to it by helping human resource managers identify specialized agencies, journals, and newsletters where recruitment ads and position announcements might attract the best-qualified applicants. Broad dissemination of the position announcement by the human resource department is critical in order to comply with merit system provisions. This process may include a specialized advertising strategy to contact universities, professional societies, and special employment registers, or to use publications that reach minorities, women, disabled persons, and Vietnam War veterans.

Department managers also assist the recruitment effort through disseminating letters or announcements to colleagues in the field and soliciting similar assistance from current employees. Managers often recruit at professional meetings or conferences as well as at high school and college career days. To aid in attracting potential applicants, some police and fire departments schedule open houses and invite the public to tour the facilities and talk to supervisors and employees about career opportunities.

TESTING AND SELECTION

The focus of job-related testing and selection is on the identification of the content of the job itself as a basis for developing test or selection criteria. The legal impetus for job-related selection in the public sector began with the merit system. The focus of this system was to select individuals for public service based on ability and fitness for the position and not on subjective criteria or other extraneous factors such as political affiliation.

With the advent of Equal Employment Opportunity/Affirmative Action (EEO/AA) laws and guidelines, job-related selection criteria became a significant focus once again. Since these laws are still in force in many public sector jurisdictions, human resource and department managers are required to adhere to these provisions. Table 2-2 provides an overview of the major EEO/AA regulations that impact the area of testing and selection. These regulations include Title VII of the Civil Rights Act of 1964 as amended, the Age Discrimination in Employment Act of 1967 as amended, the Americans with Disabilities Act of 1990 (ADA), the Civil Rights Act of 1991, and the Uniform Guidelines on Employee Selection Procedures 1978. Title VII of the Civil Rights Act as amended in 1972 by the Equal Employment Opportunity Act requires employment neutrality or nondiscrimination in human resource practices regardless of race, color, religion, sex, national origin, or disability. The Age Discrimination in Employment Act of 1967 and its amendments prohibit employers from discriminating against individuals of ages forty and over. The Americans with Disabilities Act of 1990 prohibits discrimination against applicants and employees with disabilities in matters of employment and the Rehabilitation Act of 1973 protects federal employees with disabilities. Monetary damages in cases of intentional discrimination can be sought under the provisions of the Civil Rights Act of 1991.[10] Further discussion of the impact of EEO/AA requirements on job classification and pay, performance appraisal, and grievance procedures can be found in Chapters 3, 4, and 5, respectively.

The Uniform Guidelines provide a specific definition of test and selection procedures, and they reinforce the laws and court decisions which mandate

TABLE 2-2	EQUAL EMPLOYMENT OPPORTUNITY AND AFFIRMATIVE ACTION EMPLOYMENT REQUIREMENTS	
Human Resource Factors	**EEO/AA Requirements for Employers**	**Legislation, Regulations, Guidelines**
Overall Employment Practices	Prohibit employment discrimination based on race, color, religion, sex, national origin, or disability	Title VII of the Civil Rights Act of 1964 Civil Rights Act of 1991 Rehabilitation Act of 1973 Title I of the Americans with Disabilities Act of 1990 State and local laws
Recruitment	Prohibit employment discrimination of persons aged forty and older	Age Discrimination in Employment Act of 1967 as amended Executive Orders 11246 and 11375 Revised Order 4 as amended Federal, state, or local contracts
Testing	Conduct extended search beyond traditional sources Demonstrate job-relatedness, validity, and absence of adverse impact on protected classes	Executive Orders 11246 and 11375 Revised Order 4 as amended Uniform Guidelines on Employee Selection Procedures of 1978
Selection	Use goals and timetables to select employees based on an analysis of protected classes' representation in the workforce/labor force compared to utilization of protected classes in the organization to provide balanced representation	Executive Orders 11246 and 11375 Revised Order 4 as amended Uniform Guidelines on Employee Selection Procedures of 1978
Performance Appraisal	Demonstrate job-relatedness, validity, and absence of adverse impact on protected classes	Uniform Guidelines on Employee Selection Procedures

that tests must be job-related. Under the Guidelines, a test or selection procedure is defined as

> Any measure, combination of measures, or procedure used as a basis for any employment decision. Selection procedures include the full range of assessment techniques from traditional paper and pencil tests, performance tests, training programs, or probationary periods and physical, educational and work experience requirements through informal or casual interviews and unscored application forms.[11]

This covers virtually any process used to screen and evaluate applicants.

To add impetus to these laws, in the 1971 case of *Griggs v Duke Power and Light Co.* (401 U.S. 424 [1971]), the Supreme Court confirmed that only job-related criteria should be used in the testing and selection process. Griggs was an African-American who found that he could not qualify for a job as a supervisor of ditch digging at Duke Power and Light because he had to have a high school diploma and do well on the Minnesota Achievement Test. Griggs questioned what the relationship was between the test criteria and his ability to do the job. It was argued that African-Americans as a group possessed disproportionately fewer high school diplomas and performed significantly below the norm on the achievement test due to a pattern of educational, social, and economic discrimination. The Supreme Court agreed with Griggs that there should be a statistically valid relationship between the selection criteria and job performance. Because Duke Power and Light was unable to demonstrate that the ability to supervise others digging a ditch increased markedly with the possession of a high school diploma, the *criterion validity* standard could not be met.

Whether or not affirmative action remains lawful in public sector organizations, the intent of the Uniform Guidelines and cases such as *Griggs v Duke Power* reinforce two of the major tenets of the merit principles—realistic standards and absence of discrimination. These principles compel public organizations to use qualification standards that are reasonably related to the job to be filled, and to assure that these standards contain factors that relate only to ability and fitness for employment. Excessive qualification requirements or subjective factors such as personal lifestyle, height, weight, and appearance should not be a part of the selection process.

Once appropriate qualification requirements for a position are established, the human resource department administers and evaluates various combinations of tests. Such tests or screening processes include application forms or résumés, written examinations, performance tests (e.g., operation of equipment), interviews, and assessment centers.

APPLICATION/RÉSUMÉ SCREENING. There are two basic ways to screen initial applicants. One approach is to *screen out* as many candidates as possible so that the field of applicants is narrowed to those who meet the highest levels of experience and education. The alternative approach is to *screen in* as many qualified candidates as possible who meet the minimum job requirements. By being as inclusive as possible, human resource departments have more work to do in assessing candidates, but the department manager will have the advantage of a broader range of applicants from which to choose.

Department managers can play an important role in helping human resource managers determine who should be screened in. Let us imagine for the moment that the water utilities division has a vacancy for a customer service representative, someone who will answer customer questions at a high-traffic front counter. Due to mergers and downsizing, there is a flood of applications from former bank tellers who list experience as customer service representatives. They have no knowledge about water utilities, much less the public sector. Since the job announcement only mentions demonstrated interpersonal skills, are they qualified? The department manager can help the human resource specialist determine if specific experience in water utilities is required or whether transferable skills are sufficient. A more inclusive screening would qualify the former bank tellers; a more exclusive approach would screen them out.

Whether department managers are involved as participants in reviewing applications and résumés or are simply assisting the human resource specialist in defining the screening criteria, the criteria for evaluating candidates should focus only on job-related experience, education, and training as delineated in the position announcement. Legal problems often occur when managers deviate from the requirements, apply them unevenly to candidates, or ask impermissible questions. Guidelines for permissible preemployment inquiries are delineated in Appendix A. These guidelines apply to both the application screening and interviews.

WRITTEN TESTS. The department manager can serve as a subject matter expert for the human resource department in the development of written test content. For example, if the position being filled is a social worker who investigates allegations of child abuse and neglect, the department manager might suggest to the human resource specialist that the key areas to test are risk assessment, crisis intervention, and brief therapies. On the other hand, if the social worker position being filled is in mental health, the test content may be quite different—knowledge of the diagnostic categories of mental illness described in the *Diagnostic and Statistical Manual IV* (*DSM-IV*), psychiatric treatment modalities, and discharge planning.

Department managers can also help human resource specialists develop simulation questions to determine how appropriate the response of the applicant for the position of social worker would be to a typical but hypothetical workplace situation. For example, a social worker has been assigned to follow up on a client who has been discharged home. Upon arrival at the house, the social worker, who speaks only English, discovers that the client speaks only Spanish. How could the social worker communicate effectively with this client?

Managers can also help human resource specialists to establish rating scales and the relative weight that should be given responses to written questions. For example, in the above hypothetical situation the respondent could be rated not only on the communication method proposed but also on the respondent's sensitivity to cultural issues. Using an uncertified translator would be inappropriate if legal matters were at stake, using a neighbor might breach confidentiality, and having a spouse translate may violate cultural norms.

For the most part, the use of subject matter experts lends credibility to the testing process by suggesting that the content of the test is valid. However, it should be kept in mind that *content validity* is not the same as *criterion validity*. A written test should be valid in terms of its content and in its adherence to the appropriate criteria. The validity standards for content and criteria are not always the same, and developers of tests must be careful. Content validity is often a subjective judgment whereas criterion validity can be determined only by statistical analysis.

THE INTERVIEW.   The department manager or supervisor may be involved at the qualifying or panel interview stage and is usually the primary interviewer of the top candidates. As indicated by the previous definition, the interview is also a test and must be job-related as well as validated. As in the written test process, the human resource and department managers typically work together to assure that the interview questions meet these requirements.

When developing job-related interview questions, the human resource manager should utilize

a. a comprehensive position description;

b. the qualification requirements for the position including the knowledge, skills, abilities, education, and experience expected;

c. a structured and written set of interview questions based on items *a* and *b* above; and

d. a system for scoring the candidates' answers.

Most oral examinations follow a structured interview format. That is, to ensure uniformity and fairness, the same questions are asked of each interviewee. Substitute questions or major variations on the theme are not allowed. To ensure consistency, raters are often taught how to score candidate answers.

Table 2-3 provides an example of the development of job-related interview questions. In the example, one major duty of a social worker is to determine clients' eligibility for services. The *qualification requirement* states that successful candidates for this position must have knowledge of the state eligibility regulations, knowledge of available services, and the ability to screen applications for services. Applicants are given a situational *interview question* to test their knowledge involving an eligibility problem that they would encounter on a regular basis. The human resource manager may provide interviewers with *criteria for evaluation* of the respondents' answers so they know the elements of an acceptable answer. A typical interview includes one or more questions for each job or qualification requirement that interviewers intend to test.

PERFORMANCE TESTS.   Another job-related selection technique is a performance test. It has tended to be underutilized in the public sector because it creates logistical problems. Performance tests are simulations that require the applicant to demonstrate a skill or job knowledge to the evaluator. The human resource department and department manager can review the critical duties and requirements of a position to determine whether there are elements that can be observed and rated using a structured demonstration.

Performance tests can be used alone or in combination with other approaches to help a manager or supervisor make better employment decisions

| TABLE 2-3 | DEVELOPMENT OF JOB-RELATED INTERVIEW QUESTIONS |

Position: Social Service Worker

Task/Duty	Qualification Requirements	Interview Question	Criteria for Evaluation
Determine clients' eligibility for services	Knowledge of state eligibility regulations; knowledge of available services; ability to screen applications	You have thoroughly reviewed a client's paperwork and con-ducted an interview. It is clear that the client is in critical need of the services but will not meet the eligibility requirements for another month. How will you handle this situation with the applicant?	The applicant's response should contain the follow-ing components: (1) an explanation of the regulations to the client concerning the eligibility period; (2) referrals to other known services and agencies for tempo-rary assistance; (3) establishment of another appointment for the applicant to return when he/she is eligible.

about an applicant's ability to perform the job. For example, candidates for faculty positions in state universities may be required to teach a class session; fire and police candidates might perform physical agility and endurance tests; trainers could demonstrate their interpersonal and presentation skills. For jobs that require the employee to operate equipment, human resource specialists may test the applicant's ability to follow a series of instructions while using a machine. Computer programmers may be given a programming exercise to demonstrate their expertise on a given computer system; or ac-counting technicians may be asked to prepare a trial balance on an electronic spreadsheet.

ASSESSMENT CENTERS. Assessment centers engage candidates in a simu-lation of representative work activities, usually of a managerial nature. For example, candidates for a fire captain position may be asked to prioritize sev-eral projects that have been placed in his or her in-basket (this is known as an in-basket exercise), to demonstrate leadership, negotiation, and oral skills in a leaderless group discussing budgetary priorities, to give a speech on fire prevention, and to display appropriate discipline techniques in a perfor-mance evaluation role play. Studies indicate that this form of testing provides a valid means to evaluate candidates and is more likely than traditional se-lection processes to produce fairer employment and promotion decisions for women and minorities.[12] Other studies indicate serious flaws in the process as it pertains to the public sector. In stating his purposes for the study, Lowry points to a continuing concern for the validity of the assessment center process. While there have been questions raised about the validity of the assessment center, an overwhelming body of literature shows a positive relationship between assessment center scores and performance as a manager or supervisor. On the other hand, it has been found that validity is affected by the way a center is conducted, the selection of assessors, and related issues.[13]

Department managers commonly play several roles when assessment centers are used to select candidates. They may work with the human resource specialist to develop the job-related content of the assessment center exercises, develop rating criteria, train assessment center raters on the selection criteria, or serve as assessment center raters themselves.

THE PROBATIONARY PERIOD. Although most department managers do not realize it, probationary periods are also considered tests within the definition of the test/selection procedure in the Uniform Guidelines. The probationary period is the ultimate test of the selection process and, not unexpectedly, must meet the requirements of any other test. Most public sector organizations reserve the right to dismiss an employee during this period without the due process rights that are generally afforded permanent or tenured employees. Despite these provisions, employers must still demonstrate that any termination was valid, job-related, and absent of adverse impact. If challenged by a member of a protected class, department and human resource managers must answer to the EEOC or to any other compliance agency with jurisdiction and enforcement power.

Probationary periods generally range from six months to one year and allow the department manager an opportunity to determine whether the new employee meets an expected level of competency. This is typically accomplished through a series of oral and written performance appraisals. It is critical for both the manager and the probationary employee to view this time as an extension of the testing period and to clearly identify the duties, standards of performance, and expectations for the position (see Chapter 4 for further discussion of performance appraisal). Although many public managers may treat the probationary period as pro forma, it really is the true test of whether a new employee is the "right person" for the job.

OTHER EMPLOYMENT REGULATIONS

In addition to recruitment, testing and selection, and performance appraisal, there are several other significant aspects of employment that are covered by legislation, regulations, and guidelines. As outlined in Table 2-4, these include job classification and pay, grievance procedures, placement and assignments, training, nepotism, benefits, family leave, and disability accommodation.

Placement, assignment, and training are particularly important areas for managers with regard to EEO/AA. It is essential for the manager to provide equal opportunity for minorities and women to participate in training

TABLE 2-4	OTHER EMPLOYMENT REGULATIONS	
Human Resource Factor	**Employer's Requirements**	**Legislation, Regulations, Guidelines**
Job Classification and Pay	Provide equal pay for equal work to women and men who perform substantially equal work	Equal Pay Act of 1963 Revised Order 4 as amended Fair Labor Standards Act
Grievance Procedures	Provide a process for grieving discrimination issues	Revised Order 4 as amended
Placement and Assignments	Provide opportunities for protected classes to receive assignments that lead to upward mobility or learning experiences	Revised Order 4 as amended
Training	Develop training to improve areas of overconcentration of women and minorities (e.g., clerical or maintenance positions); provide equal opportunity to receive training	Revised Order 4 as amended
Nepotism	Adopt policy that does not discriminate against women	Title VII of the Civil Rights Act of 1964
Benefits	Provide benefit programs that do not discriminate against women and minorities	Equal Pay Act of 1963 Revised Order 4 as amended
Family Leave	Provide unpaid leave to women and men employees for the birth of a child, to care for a seriously ill family member, or for the employee's own serious illness; treat pregnancy like any other temporary disability with regard to compensation, leave, and benefits	Family and Medical Leave Act of 1993 Title VII of the Civil Rights Act of 1964 Revised Order 4 as amended
Disability Accommodation	Provide reasonable accommodation for persons with disabilities	Rehabilitation Act of 1973 Americans with Disabilities Act of 1990

or conferences, to receive appointments to high-status committees, and to work on special projects or temporary assignments. These situations, which provide vital experience and exposure for present and future job opportunities, should be available to all employees.

EEO/AA regulations provide protection against discrimination in the provision of benefits, based on gender or race. This protection includes the provision of medical, hospital, accident, and life insurance, paid and unpaid leave, bonuses, and retirement benefits. Although the human resource department usually handles the administration of such benefits, employees often have questions about them for their department managers. Therefore, the department manager must be knowledgeable about the equitable application of these policies.

For example, Tom asks his supervisor if he can have family leave because his wife is about to have twins and she will need help during the first month. They also have another child under the age of five. Tom is an exceptional worker and his absence will adversely affect the productivity of the unit. Clearly a woman is entitled to pregnancy and family leave, but is a man?

The answer is yes! The Family and Medical Leave Act of 1993 allows men and women employees leave for birth of a child. In addition, women affected by pregnancy, childbirth, or related medical conditions shall be treated the same as employees with any other temporary disability.[14] Under Title VII, child-care leaves are treated on the same basis as other nonmedical leaves such as travel or education leaves and should be made available to male and female employees.

Chad is Maria's supervisor. They enjoy each other's company and eventually marry. Although there is no evidence of favoritism, others in the workplace are complaining that Maria has an unfair advantage and will get undeserved promotions, easier work assignments, and more favorable performance appraisals. Since Maria earns the lesser income and is considering leaving her job to raise a family, can she be asked to resign or accept a transfer?

Nepotism or antinepotism rules that have a disparate impact on women are unlawful. An employer cannot have a rule that always requires the female spouse to resign if two employees marry. The organization can, however, refuse to place one spouse under the direct supervision of the other or to place both spouses in the same department, division, or facility. If coworkers marry, the regulations require the employer to make reasonable efforts to assign job duties to minimize problems of supervision, safety, security, and morale.[15] Thus, the decision about which spouse is reassigned rests primarily on the couple and on the employer's ability to make reasonable accommodations.

The intent of the legislation, regulations, and guidelines in these areas is to assure that protected classes (i.e., minorities, women, and disabled persons) are equitably represented in the workforce and positive efforts are made to provide fair, job-related appraisals of their performance; that they are given opportunities for work experiences and training that will help with advancement; and that they are not discriminated against in the areas of benefits, leaves, and nepotism policies.

Sexual orientation is a civil rights and workplace diversity issue that is not yet covered by federal law though legislation is pending in Congress. Anti-discrimination laws and employee benefits policies are being implemented at the state and local levels. According to Gardenswartz and Rowe,

> Nine states (California, Connecticut, Hawaii, Massachusetts, Minnesota, New Jersey, Rhode Island, Vermont, and Wisconsin) include gays in civil rights protection

that extends to employment. Another 15 to 18 states include some degree of gay rights in executive orders and 87 cities and counties have civil rights ordinances for gays.[16]

The trend toward protecting the rights of gay and lesbian workers is increasing steadily among states and localities and in public and private sector organizations within their jurisdictions. Along with the recognition of rights, a number of organizations are adopting domestic partner benefits that cover an employee's partner in a same-sex relationship. Among the types of benefits offered to domestic partners are health insurance, pension plans, relocation expense reimbursement, tuition discounts, and bereavement leave.[17]

WORKSHOP 2

Job-Related Testing

PRE-SERVICE STUDENTS

Objective or Subjective?

The development of selection devices that assess the qualifications of an applicant in an objective fashion is difficult. The goal of this exercise is to improve the ability of students to identify objective, job-related selection criteria. To prepare for this exercise and gather additional information, students may wish to refer to Appendix A: Preemployment Inquiry Guidelines, *The Dictionary of Occupational Titles,* or job announcements and qualification requirements for public-agency positions advertised online.

Instructions:

- Divide the class into four groups.
- Two "research" teams will compete against each other.
- Two "contestant" teams will compete against each other.

Pregame Activities:

Research Teams:
1. Each of the research teams will develop a list of objective and subjective selection devices, including but not limited to

  - interview questions
  - performance test items
  - aptitude test items
  - educational qualifications
  - experience qualifications
  - training qualifications

2. Each selection device must be tied to a particular position (such as librarian or computer analyst), which is identified and studied by the research team.

3. The members of the team must reach consensus on whether the item is objective or subjective.

4. Each research team should develop about twenty-five questions.

5. The research teams are given different color 3 x 5 cards.

6. Each question is placed on a 3 x 5 card in the following format:

At the top of the card: "For the position of _____, is the following item an objective or subjective selection device? _____"

The answer at the bottom of the card.

Contestant Teams:

1. The contestant teams should be kept separate from each other and the research teams so that they do not overhear the questions and answers.

2. Each contestant team shall select a team leader.

3. Each of the contestant teams can prepare themselves by

- developing a definition of what is objective/subjective selection criteria

- discussing examples of objective/subjective selection devices they have experienced

- reviewing Appendix A: Preemployment Inquiry Guidelines

- holding a mock contest

The Contest:

1. The moderator collects the cards from each research team.

2. A coin is flipped to see which contestant team goes first.

3. The moderator then presents the questions, alternating between those submitted from research teams "A" and "B."

4. Each contestant team has thirty seconds to respond. The decision of the team leader is final.

5. Each contestant team continues to answer questions until they answer incorrectly. One point is awarded for each correct answer.

Protest:

1. The contestant team leader may protest an answer.

2. The protesting contestant team has a total of three minutes to argue why the answer should be changed.

3. The research team that wrote the question has a maximum of three minutes to defend its question and answer.

4. The classroom instructor serves as the judge.

5. If the judge rules in favor of the protesting contestant team, it is awarded two points and the research team loses two points. If the judge rules in favor of the research team, the research team gains two points and the protesting team loses two points.

Determining the "Champs":

1. The research teams earn points for stumping the "contestant" teams. The research team with the most points is the "research champ."
2. The contestant team earns points for correct answers. The contestant team with the most correct responses is the "contestant champ."
3. The overall winner is the team that has the most points.

IN-SERVICE STUDENTS

Instructions:

Form groups of approximately five members. In each group, have each employed group member briefly describe his or her position. Select one member's position as a focus for this workshop. Alternatively, group members may invite a guest to the workshop whose job is of interest to the class.

Workshop Project:

Have the selected individual describe three of his or her most important job duties. Then have him or her describe the accompanying qualification requirements (i.e., knowledge, skills, abilities, education, and type and years of experience) for each duty. The group should discuss and identify the most appropriate type of test (e.g., application form/résumé, written test, performance test, interview, and/or assessment center) for each qualification requirement in order to evaluate whether a job applicant is qualified for this position. Once the type of test has been identified, the group should develop a sample test question or item for each qualification requirement related to the job duties.

NOTES

1. William Claiborne, "California Ban on Affirmative Action Cleared," *Washington Post*, 28 August 1997, A01.

2. Tom Brune and Joe Heim, "Initiative 200—New Battle Begins: Interpreting the Law," *The Seattle Times*, 4 November 1998, B1.

3. Norma M. Riccucci, "Will Affirmative Action Survive into the Twenty-first Century?" in *Public Personnel Management: Current Concerns, Future Challenges*, eds. Carolyn Ban and Norma M. Riccucci (New York: Longman, 1997), 69.

4. Ann G. Sjoerdsma, "Educational 'Diversity' Under Attack," *The Baltimore Sun*, 26 March 2000, 1C.

5. Riccucci, "Affirmative Action," 68.

6. Joan E. Pynes, ed., *Human Resources Management for Public and Nonprofit Organizations* (San Francisco: Jossey-Bass, 1997), 30–31.

7. Tamu Chambers and Norma M. Riccucci, "Models of Excellence in Workplace Diversity," in *Public Personnel Management: Current Concerns, Future Challenges,* eds. Carolyn Ban and Norma M. Riccucci (New York: Longman, 1997), 89.

8. "Unleashing the Power of Your Workforce," IPMA [database online] (Alexandria, VA: IPMA [cited 8 March 2000]), member-restricted access from http://www.ipma.org.

9. Gill R. Hickman and Ann Creighton-Zollar, "Diverse Self-Directed Work Teams: Developing Strategic Initiatives for Twenty-first Century Organizations," *Public Personnel Management* 27 (summer 1998): 190–191.

10. A summary of these laws and questions and answers about job discrimination can be found in U.S. Equal Employment Opportunity Commission, "Federal Laws Prohibiting Job Discrimination Questions and Answers," http://www.eeoc.gov/facts.

11. U.S. Equal Employment Opportunity Commission, "Uniform Guidelines on Employee Selection Procedures," *Federal Register,* vol. 43, pt. 4, sec. 16, 25 August 1978.

12. John A. Hamman and Uday Desai, "Current Issues in Recruitment and Selection," in *Public Personnel Administration: Problems and Prospects,* eds. Steven W. Hays and Richard C. Kearney (Englewood Cliffs, NJ: Prentice Hall, 1995), 87.

13. Phillip E. Lowry, "A Survey of the Assessment Center Process in the Public Sector," *Public Personnel Management* 25 (summer 1996): 315.

14. U.S. Department of Labor, Wage and Hour Division, "Family Medical Leave Act as Revised 7-1-98," *Code of Federal Regulations,* Title 29, vol 3., pts. 500–899, pp. 775–787.

15. Richard Simmons, *Employment Discrimination and EEO Practice Manual* (Van Nuys, CA: Castle, 1996), 247–248, 269.

16. Lee Gardenswartz and Anita Rowe, "Diversity Q&A: How Do I Balance the Rights of All Employees When Accommodating Gays and Lesbians in the Workforce?," in Society for Human Resource Management [database online] (Alexandria, VA: Society for Human Resource Management [cited 8 March 2000]), member-restricted access from http://www.shrm.org.

17. Patricia Digh, "In and out of the Corporate Closet," in Society for Human Resource Management [database online] (Alexandria, VA: Society for Human Resource Management [cited 19 March 2000]), member-restricted access from http://www.shrm.org.

3

POSITION MANAGEMENT: UNDERSTANDING THE EMPLOYEE'S JOB

In most public organizations, the human resource department has the primary responsibility for writing job descriptions, setting minimum qualifications for positions, and determining suitable compensation in a structured classification system. On the front line, however, the department manager determines the specific job duties and how knowledge, skills, and abilities are applied to the job at hand. The department manager monitors the effort each employee expends and recommends actual compensation for each individual worker.

When department managers do not have, or do not utilize, the human resource specialist's expertise, employee morale may suffer and grievances may result. Managing positions in the department is critical to a manager's ability to maximize the productivity of employees and the unit as a whole. Too often changes occur in employees' positions by accident rather than as a planned strategy for position management. For example, because of a certain talent displayed or simply because they are in the right place at the right time, workers sometimes find themselves performing duties outside their original job classification. While they may initially enjoy the challenge of new responsibilities and novel work assignments, they may eventually become dissatisfied if there is insufficient recognition and reward for their efforts.

Lack of planning is also a problem when managers immediately fill a vacant position before enough thought is given to whether the position is really needed, or whether it should be restructured. In order to develop a planned position management strategy, department managers must know the duties, responsibilities, and qualification requirements of each position, and how they want to utilize each position within the unit. To make effective use of the positions available requires an understanding of the job analysis process, the elements of a comprehensive position description, and the rationale underlying classification systems.

DEFINING JOB ANALYSIS

A job analysis is a systematic process of collecting data for determining the knowledge, skills, abilities, and other characteristics (KSAOCs) required to successfully perform a job and to make judgements about the nature of a specific job. A job analysis identifies a job's activities, behaviors, tasks, and performance standards, the context in which the job is performed, and the personal requirements necessary to perform a job, such as personality, interests, physical characteristics, aptitudes, and job-related knowledge and skills. Each position is also analyzed in regard to its relationship to other positions in the organization.[1]

By analyzing what jobholders do and determining what functions are critical to accomplish the organization's mission, job analysis can (and should) play an important role in reengineering today's workplace so that human resources are effectively and efficiently utilized. "Right-sizing" can avoid the adverse impacts of downsizing by making sure that every position is essential, work is evenly distributed, and workers are properly trained.

JOB ANALYSIS AND DEVELOPMENT OF THE POSITION DESCRIPTION

A thorough, complete job analysis is one of the keys to effective position management. Clearly identifying the duties and responsibilities of a job tends to preclude duplication of effort, and it may help avoid unrealistic expectations by workers and managers. Such an analysis can greatly assist a manager who is trying to decide if an employee or an applicant is qualified to perform the job. Sometimes a job analysis can lead to highlighting specific areas in which additional training might be needed.

There are also legal reasons for doing a job analysis. Conducting a job analysis is one of the ways an organization can tell if it is meeting legal requirements or needs to make changes to avoid possible litigation.

■ Until the passage of the Classification Act in 1923, there was no necessary correspondence between one's job title, duty, or pay. The Classification Act became the initial federal government model for aligning job titles and pay scales with standardized categories of duties and responsibilities. The act established a uniform classification system so that government employees with comparable duties would be paid similarly. A job analysis determines how similar or dissimilar these duties are and provides justification for one's classification system.

■ Title VII of the Civil Rights Act of 1964 encourages organizations to do a job analysis so that selection, retention, and promotion are based upon objective job factors rather than subjective feelings and attitudes. A job analysis identifies essential job functions, performance standards, and minimum knowledge, skills, and abilities to perform the work activities. If the civil service examination, performance evaluation system, and promotional examination are based upon such a job analysis, managers have established a solid foundation to defend their decisions.

- The Occupational Safety and Health Act passed in 1970 requires employers to inform workers of potential workplace safety and health hazards. Sharing the position description (one of the by-products of a job analysis) with workers can meet the "right-to-know" requirement. A proper job analysis can address the physical work conditions as well as the training needed to be proficient with certain equipment.

- The Americans with Disabilities Act of 1990 requires that employers make reasonable accommodations for disabled applicants and employees. Reasonable accommodation may mean that the employer purchases special reading machines for the visually impaired, special amplification and TTY telephones for the hearing impaired, or special office equipment for the physically challenged. The only time that the employer need not make reasonable accommodations is when there is an economic hardship on the organization (an unlikely scenario in large public organizations) or the person would not be able to perform the essential functions of the job even with reasonable accommodations. The job analysis determines which work activities are essential and what physical requirements are needed for each position or classification.

- Finally, in locations where collective bargaining occurs, union representatives are likely to argue for clear definitions of duties and responsibilities so that union members will be duly compensated for working outside the normal scope of their duties. Grievances over the scope of one's duties can more easily be settled if a job analysis has been done.

JOB ANALYSIS METHODS

Information for a job analysis is gathered in a variety of ways. A list of work activities can be acquired easily from old job descriptions available through one's own human resource department, a human resource department in an adjoining organization, or even gathered from a government documents library.[2] Existing performance appraisal forms also supply information about job expectations and standards. Training manuals and documents give additional clues about what a position encompasses.

Information can also be gathered from subject matter experts (SMEs). In some cases, the SME is the person actually doing the job. At other times, the SME might be the immediate supervisor who has a better idea about the scope of the job across several workers, or a consultant who has had the time to study similar jobs in other settings. Certain unions, professions, and professional organizations consider themselves to be SMEs. Certified public accountants, for example, have developed extensive documentation about performance standards and licensing requirements.

Besides the aforementioned techniques, human resource specialists may also use a desk audit, a position questionnaire, or a critical incident approach. A desk audit is the direct observation of the person doing the job. It is often used to identify work activities not identified in the preliminary information-gathering phase, and it frequently reveals discrepancies between what workers think they do and what they actually do. While not a substitute for a desk audit, a position questionnaire is frequently used to gather information over a broad range of jobs in different settings. The information obtained is of a more quantitative than qualitative nature, although the two are not necessarily mutually exclusive. A position questionnaire is sent periodically to jobholders. It contains standard questions such as what equipment do you normally use, how much must you lift, what proportion of the job is sitting/standing, how much physical exertion is required, to whom do you report, what job categories do you supervise, and so on. The most important questions are those having to do with identifying major work activities and the percentage of time spent on each.

If the human resource specialist is fairly familiar with the position being analyzed, or if there is insufficient time to apply the other methods previously mentioned, the critical incident method may be appropriate. The human resource specialist reviews records kept on critical incidents to learn the key work activities of the position. For example, a review of safety records can indicate which work activities need to be performed precisely. Likewise, a review of child deaths would inform a child protective services administrator about inadequate casework methods or lax supervision. A subsequent probe might produce crucial data on the essential steps in a child-abuse investigation.

The end result of the information-gathering process is a written position description. Appendix B contains a sample position description form. Position descriptions usually contain the following information:

- job title (or class series);
- definition—a brief summary of duties and responsibilities, what position one reports to, the number and type of people supervised (if any), level of decision-making authority;
- essential work activities;
- working conditions—for example, level of person-to-person contact, health and safety hazards, and physical exertion required; and
- qualification requirements—minimum level of knowledge, skills, and abilities, personal attributes (aptitude, temperament, interests, originality, and creativity), certificates, and so forth.

Department managers should have a position description for each position supervised. Effective position management requires that department managers review the position description regularly to compare actual work activities with those described on paper. A discrepancy could indicate that the essential duties of a position have shifted, perhaps necessitating a further job analysis to determine if a job should be reclassified.

CLASSIFICATION, REALLOCATION, AND UPWARD MOBILITY

The classification process is perhaps one of the most misunderstood among human resource procedures because of its technical nature and the complexity of the analysis process. A request for reallocation (or reclassification) is one of the most frequent requests received by a department manager concerning an employee's job. Unfortunately, it is often requested for inappropriate reasons such as rewarding longevity or outstanding performance rather than to reclassify a job because the job duties have changed substantially.

The classification/reallocation process involves an intricate balance of responsibilities and activities involving the department head, the human resource department, and the employee.

POSITION CLASSIFICATION

Many public sector organizations use the conventional position-classification method of job evaluation. Position classification is the process of grouping jobs together based on similar duties, responsibilities, and qualification requirements.[3] It provides the foundation for "equal pay for equal work" which evolved as a result of the focus on objective job content and pay practices under the merit principles. As indicated earlier, the 1923 Classification Act was reinforced by the Equal Pay Act of 1963 and Title VII of the Civil Rights Act of 1964, which prohibit wage discrimination based on sex.

The position classification process compares a specific job against an established standard or specification. The *Dictionary of Occupational Titles* published by the Department of Labor classifies twelve thousand job titles using a nine-digit code system that identifies the major occupational group and how that job relates to data, people, and things.

In smaller organizations, one is likely to find a classification standard system that easily translates into a position description and job announcement. The position classification process form in Appendix B is used to compare positions across eight job factors:

- nature and variety of work;
- type of guidelines available;
- type of supervision received;
- decision-making authority;
- originality or creativity;

- person-to-person contact;
- supervision over others; and
- qualification requirements.

The sample guideline in Appendix B provides a brief description of these eight factors. The advantages of the position-classification system are that the eight factors provide a standardized method for comparing jobs within and across classifications and that the system is well known and widely used in the public sector. The major disadvantages are that this method requires considerable training and experience and that the analysis process and subsequent results are often difficult to explain to department managers and employees, particularly when the outcome does not support the classification level requested by the department manager or employee.

POINT-FACTOR CLASSIFICATION METHODS. A popular system, point-factor classification, breaks jobs into their component parts. A certain number of points are assigned to each factor depending on its relative importance. The more complex and responsible duties of a position are awarded higher points. Generally, the higher the point total, the more complex the job. Through detailed job analysis, factors such as education, working conditions, physical demands, responsibility, decision-making authority, and skill level are reviewed when utilizing this method. Once this information is obtained, the factors are divided into degrees. The more progressive the degree, the greater the points on that factor. Utilizing this method affords employers the opportunity to break jobs down into several compensable factors.[4]

There are advantages and disadvantages to utilizing the point-factor classification method. Department managers and employees find it easier to understand or more equitable than the position classification method. Once established, the plan is relatively simple to administer. The major disadvantage is that developing the initial factors and point system can be complex and partially subjective.

BROADBANDING CLASSIFICATION METHOD. Broadbanding, sometimes called career banding, involves combining or clustering several related job levels and functions into a larger category known as a band.[5] This method began as a compensation innovation but has evolved into a career development system and, according to LeBlanc and Ellis, is a way of managing an organization's human resources.[6] For example, an employer may elect to reduce as many as two-thirds of its classification and salary levels into as few as five to ten bands. This system allows managers and employees more flexibility, more opportunities for employee development and advancement, and more possibilities for using employee capacity and skills in a wider range of situations and assignments. These advantages reflect some of the requisite changes that are needed when organizations move to flatter structures, more person-based systems, and employee empowerment.

The federal government pioneered broadbanding in the public sector on a limited basis beginning in 1980 and several state and local governments have adopted or are moving toward broadbanding, including California, Michigan, Minnesota, Wisconsin, the City of Charlotte, North Carolina, and the City of Virginia Beach, Virginia.[7] Although several federal agencies continue to use this new method, the use of broadbanding in the federal government is currently limited to demonstration projects and agencies exempt from Title 5 U.S.C.[8]

The process begins with a job analysis. After the analysis is done, jobs are assigned to career paths based on similarity of job requirements, and four or five bands are chosen. The new classification system is based on fewer factors, typically six or fewer rather than the traditional eight to nine.[9] The trend toward broadbanding is likely to continue because of the streamlined nature of the system, its flexibility, and its apparent compatibility with the direction of public sector organizations toward person-based systems and flatter structures.

There are some problems associated with broadbanding. Most organizations are accustomed to having more distinct boundaries within their classification and pay system and are uncomfortable with the vagueness associated with broadbanding. In some settings, there may be resistance to a new set of rules and pay structure. Therefore employers need to be aware that there is the potential for all employees to float to the maximum, which for any number of jobs in the band would be much higher than market value. A publication by the International Personnel Management Association (IPMA) has summarized strengths and weaknesses of the system as follows.

Broadbanding Strengths
- Provides a simplified, more flexible compensation and job evaluation system
- Facilitates pay for performance and competency-based pay
- Supports dual career ladders for technical experts and supervisors
- Facilitates employee career development and lateral mobility
- Supports more flexible and less hierarchical organizations
- Aligns delayered organization with a matching pay structure

Disadvantages of Broadbanding
- Requires extensive planning, careful design, and commitment from the top
- Requires expensive communication and training
- Results in fewer vertical promotional opportunities
- May result in slower salary progression at entry level due to fewer promotions
- May make cost control more difficult as pay ranges expand

■ Requires an effective performance management system
■ Makes it more difficult to establish external pay equity due to lack of accurate salary survey data for broader job categories [10]

REALLOCATION AND UPWARD MOBILITY

Reallocation (or reclassification) is a process used to determine whether a specific job has changed significantly in terms of its duties, responsibilities, and complexity in relationship to an established standard or specification. Employees and their managers or supervisors often view reallocation as a means to gain upward mobility and increased pay. In the position management process, there are appropriate and inappropriate methods and rationales for using the reallocation process for upward mobility.

The classification or reclassification process depicted in Table 3-1 is required when there is a change in the duties and responsibilities of the position over time through job enrichment by the supervisor or by an employee who assumes more difficult or complex duties with the supervisor's explicit or implicit approval. The supervisor, employee, or human resource department can initiate the process. The employee and supervisor complete a position questionnaire about the reconfigured position. A classification analyst from the human resource department conducts a desk audit and job analysis. The final classification determination or decision is derived by comparing the factors found in the position being reviewed with the factors found in the classification standard or specification. At the end of the process, the classification analyst determines which classification best fits the position, which often results in an upward reclassification of the employee's position where appropriate. In some situations, the position is not reclassified because the new duties do not exceed the expectations of the current classification standard.

The department manager uses classification standards or specifications for several purposes:

1. to assure that he or she is using the appropriate qualification requirements when requesting that the human resource department fill a vacant position;
2. to assure that the position description contains the duties and responsibilities that are appropriate for the specific classification level of the position;
3. to help develop the performance goals, standards, and expectations for the employee's position;
4. to help determine the training needs of an employee in a specific position; and
5. to determine whether to request a position reallocation when the employee appears to be functioning at a level above his or her current classification.

| TABLE 3-1 | OVERVIEW OF CLASSIFICATION/RECLASSIFICATION PROCESS |

Task	Department Manager's and Employee's Responsibility	Human Resource Department's Responsibility
Change duties of position through:		
a. Job enrichment initiated by supervisor	X	
b. Changes in job duties initiated by employee (i.e., impact of person on job)	X	
Request for initial study or review	X	X
Completion of position questionnaire	X	
Desk audit and job analysis		X
Final classification decision		X

INAPPROPRIATE REASONS FOR REALLOCATION/RECLASSIFICATION. Decisions must be made based on actual job content using the analysis process and allocation/classification factors described in the previous section. Figure 3-1 provides a humorous representation of the inappropriate reasons that managers and employees sometimes use to request reclassification of a position.

1. Quantity of Work—The employee has been assigned an exceptional amount of work to complete, often beyond reasonable expectations.
2. Economic Problems—The employee is experiencing personal financial problems and wants an increase in salary.
3. Length of Service or Seniority—The employee has been a long-term, faithful worker but is no longer entitled to salary-step increases.
4. Time Spent at Top Salary Step—Many experienced employees have reached the top step of their salary ranges and can no longer receive salary increases other than cost-of-living raises.

Though these are compelling issues, they are unrelated to the purpose or process of reallocation and should be handled using different human resource options. The reclassification process is appropriately used under three circumstances: (a) when the employee has assumed more difficult and complex duties over a period of time (generally six months to one year) and such actions result in a change in the eight-factor analysis (i.e., impact of incumbent on the position); (b) when the supervisor purposely delegates more difficult and complex duties to the employee over a period of time in order to enhance

FIGURE 3-1 INAPPROPRIATE REASONS FOR RECLASSIFICATION

Quantity of Work

Economic Problems

Length of Service or Seniority

Time Spent at Top Salary Step

the position and create a change of classification level (i.e., a type of job enrichment); and (c) when the department or the employee eliminate key duties in the position (i.e., decrease in duties performed).

The first situation (worker assumes more difficult duties) should occur with the consent of the department manager or supervisor but often evolves by accident or out of immediate necessity. When this situation is unplanned, it can create grievances and morale problems if it is allowed to occur for long periods of time without appropriate reclassification and compensation, or without the knowledge or approval of the department head and human resource specialist. This reiterates the reason why the department head should periodically review the position description with the actual jobholder's work activities.

The second situation (supervisor delegates more tasks to worker) should occur as the result of planned job restructuring by the department manager or supervisor and should be discussed with the employee and classification analyst in the human resource department prior to implementation.

The department manager or supervisor should initiate a request for reclassification to the human resource department as the situation is developing. However, most public sector organizations also allow the employee to initiate such requests under the appropriate conditions. When a reclassification request is received, the classification analyst conducts a review using the job analysis process and renders a decision. The positive outcome of reclassification for the employee is upward mobility, which generally includes a new classification level, a change in title, and a salary increase. A negative outcome might be that the position is reclassified at a lower level.

In the third situation (worker's job duties decline), the reclassification effort sometimes, but not often, results in a downward change in classification level. This may occur for a variety of reasons, such as reorganization or restructuring of the unit, reassignment of duties by the supervisor, creation of or changes in classification standards and requirements, and relinquishment or nonperformance of duties by the employee. In these cases a classification review is conducted by the human resource department, the position is reclassified to a lower level, and the employee's salary may be red circled (i.e., frozen), until the employee leaves the position or until it is in alignment with the salary range of the new classification. For obvious reasons, employers try to avoid this situation whenever possible by reassigning the employee to another function or unit at the same classification and pay level, providing outplacement assistance, or helping the employee to correct performance problems where they exist. However, these solutions are not possible in every case.

COMPENSATION

Compensation is inherently linked to the function of classification and position management. The establishment of base compensation for positions is primarily the responsibility of the human resource department, with the exception of merit pay and noneconomic rewards. The latter are essentially administered by the department manager or supervisor and will, therefore, be the focus of this discussion along with major laws that department and human resource managers must jointly enforce.

Merit Pay or Pay-for-Performance

Originally the salary steps found in government pay ranges were intended as true merit increases to reward exceptional performance. Over time, these movements from one pay step to another became automatic increases as long as the employee was rated at a satisfactory level. The emphasis on meritorious performance was abandoned.

With the reemerging focus on individual merit in the 1970s, public sector organizations began to reintroduce merit pay or pay-for-performance plans into their compensation system.

> A pay for performance system allows organizations to design a more flexible compensation system that links performance objectives, compensation, and organizational effectiveness. According to IPMA's 1998 Compensation Survey, over half the public sector participants (54%) indicated that they compensate largely or entirely on performance.[11]

These merit pay or pay-for-performance plans require the department manager or supervisor to evaluate employees' performances and make merit pay recommendations based on established goals and standards.[12] Increases in pay are linked to outstanding or exceptional performance. Perry maintains that "for merit pay to be effective, employees must value it as a reward and expect that their effort gives them a high probability of attaining it."[13]

The Civil Service Reform Act of 1978 contained two major provisions concerning merit pay in the federal government—merit pay for managers and supervisors, and performance awards for meritorious performance in the Senior Executive Service (SES). Many local, state, and county governments as well as school districts have adopted merit pay plans. Although they are designed to help employers compensate individual merit, there have been obstacles to the successful administration of some of the programs, including those at the federal level, due to problems related to inadequate design and implementation of the performance appraisal instrument, insufficient funding, and the political issues involved in adopting pay-for-performance programs in the public sector. (See Chapter 4 for further discussion of performance appraisal instruments.)

Gainsharing is a performance-linked bonus plan for high-performing groups. Using this plan, cost savings from improved performance are shared between the organization and employees.[14] Compensation is based on the value of productivity improvement based on established measurement standards. Several public sector organizations use gainsharing programs, including Baltimore County, Maryland; City of Charlotte, North Carolina; City of Norfolk, Virginia; and City of Virginia Beach, Virginia.[15]

NONMONETARY REWARDS

Another component of employee compensation and rewards systems is the use of nonmonetary rewards. Some of these rewards can be exceptionally gratifying to employees and they can provide a means of recognizing meritorious employee performance. They are of benefit to the department manager because they cost little to implement. Examples of nonmonetary rewards include flexible working conditions and hours (e.g., telecommuting and job sharing); intrinsic rewards related to job satisfaction and content (e.g., mastering a new challenge, doing meaningful work); human interaction (e.g., project teams); individual achievement (e.g., opportunities for promotion and individual recognition); and greater autonomy (e.g., participating in the decision-making process, being delegated more responsibility and authority). Rewards that are popular with many younger workers include tangible items such as movie tickets, gift certificates for dinner, and time off.

Introducing suitable nonmonetary rewards in the workplace takes some thought, but can produce multiple benefits. Making resources available to employees not only makes their jobs easier, but also sends a message that managers recognize and support their quest to do a good job. By supplying job-related tools and equipment (such as computer software, ergonomic wrist rests, and computer reference manuals, for example), managers can keep their focus on supporting employees and improving work productivity.

Employee awards can also improve the work environment. In one national park service under the U.S. Department of Forestry, each employee has five awards per year to give to coworkers who demonstrate exceptional performance. Many state and local government offices have comparable peer awards systems. In another government office, an inexpensive, broken Grecian urn was given to the worker who had taken the most outrageous constituent complaint of the month. This symbolic reward began as a "booby prize," a joke between friends, but it soon became a morale booster that represented a unique bond between coworkers. The urn symbolized perseverance in the face of adversity while simultaneously reminding workers about work standards and expectations. With regard to the department manager, many public sector employees indicate that receiving support when needed and expressing sincere appreciation for a job well done are the most valuable rewards that they can receive. The list below includes examples of award programs that have been instituted in government agencies.

- Time off incentive awards—U.S. Department of Commerce, D.C., and City of Phoenix, Arizona
- Management awards—Hennepin County, Minnesota
- Attendance awards—City of Phoenix, Arizona

- Innovative idea award—City of Virginia Beach, Virginia, and City of Harrisonburg, Virginia
- Service awards—Town of Blacksburg, Virginia, and City of Virginia Beach, Virginia
- Safety award program—Village of Lisle, Illinois, and City of Mesa, Arizona
- Teamwork awards—City of Treasure Island, Florida, and Hennepin County, Minnesota
- Hero/valor award—On-the-Spot Award—City of Arlington, Texas, and City of Phoenix, Arizona
- Promoting diversity award—Hennepin County, Minnesota
- Customer service award—Hennepin County, Minnesota
- Peer awards—City of Virginia Beach, Virginia, and Fairfax County, Virginia
- Appreciation letters—City of Phoenix, Arizona [16]

Not understanding what kind of rewards employees seek can lead to the establishment of ineffective reward systems, create major communication problems, and produce major declines in productivity and morale. Systematic assessments and use of focus groups can identify reward systems that actually accomplish their objective, that is, to provide meaningful employee incentives that result in job satisfaction and high productivity.

OVERTIME PAY

The passage of the Fair Labor Standards Act (FLSA) in 1938, which was extended to state and local governments in 1985, required organizations to distinguish between employees who were exempt from time-and-a-half overtime pay for hours worked over forty per week from those who were nonexempt. Typically, organizations do not pay overtime to managers, but the distinction between managers and nonexempt workers is difficult to determine in some instances. Organizations must determine on a position-by-position basis which positions meet the criteria for exempt and nonexempt. Department managers must assure that the hours employees work over forty are accurately documented and submitted for overtime pay.

EQUAL PAY

The Equal Pay Act of 1963 made "equal pay for equal work" a legal requirement for women, who were often paid less than males who were doing substantially the same work. A job analysis, of course, determines if employees are doing substantially similar or comparable work. Department managers must be aware of this law when recommending starting salaries and merit pay. Considerable progress has been made to equalize salaries for women since the passage of the Equal Pay Act, although total parity has not been reached.

WORKSHOP 3

Position Management

PRE-SERVICE STUDENTS

Part 1—Job Analysis

Students will perform a desk audit and complete the Position Description form in Appendix B.

Assignment:

1. Pick a position that can be observed easily. For the purposes of this exercise, students not employed in the public sector may observe either a job in the public sector or a job on campus. Students may wish to consider asking a classmate, roommate, coworker, or parent if they can observe a typical segment of his or her workday.
2. Complete the Position Description form in Appendix B.
3. Identify the tasks, duties, and responsibilities of the job and list them on the form.

   - A *task* is the smallest unit of work and consists of several related activities. For example, a receptionist has the task of answering the phone, which consists of the following activities: answering the phone before the third ring, stating an acceptable greeting ("good morning"), stating the name of the organization, stating his/her name, and asking "How may I direct your call?" Processing the call would be a separate task that may include answering questions, transferring the call to the appropriate party, directing the call to a supervisor, providing a telephone number, and so on.
   - A *duty* consists of several different tasks performed by an individual. For example, keeping one's work area clean is a duty that consists of several different tasks—organizing the work area, putting files away, putting trash in the appropriate receptacle, cleaning up spills, and so forth.
   - Based on your observations, check whether each task or duty is performed often, occasionally, or seldom.
   - Estimate the percentage of overall time each task/duty takes.
   - Complete the rest of the form.

Comparison

A desk audit attempts to sample a typical work segment. However, unless the personnel specialist follows the employee around for some time, there are bound to be discrepancies between what the auditor thinks she/he saw and what the employee thinks she/he does. There are often disputes over the importance of a particular task and how frequently it is performed.

Interview the employee being audited. Go over your findings with the employee. On what points did you agree? On what points did you disagree?

What is the significance of doing a thorough desk audit?

Dictionary of Occupational Titles

The *Dictionary of Occupational Titles* is published by the Department of Labor and lists thousands of different occupations. The occupations are classified by how the employee relates to data, people, and things. Each occupation has a unique code.

Format:

- Go to the library and locate the *Dictionary of Occupational Titles.*
- Pick three possible jobs that you are interested in.
- Use the index to locate the page on which each job is described.
- Make a photocopy of each job.
- Highlight the nine-digit occupation code.
- Decipher the occupation code (for example, if the first digit is a zero or one, it signifies a professional, technical, or managerial occupation).
- Describe the structure of the *Dictionary of Occupational Titles.* How are jobs classified?

Part 2—Nonmonetary Rewards

The public sector often does not have the resources or the mechanisms for awarding monetary rewards. The goal of this exercise is to develop a list of possible nonmonetary rewards that could be used in the public sector.

Format:

Divide the class into small groups.

Have each group develop a list of nonmonetary rewards by exploring different resources, such as

- the Internet;
- books in the library;
- public administration and business journals in the library;
- weekly newsmagazines;
- newspapers;
- interviews of members of a professional organization such as the local International Personnel Management Association chapter, the local

International City Management Association chapter, or the local American Society for Public Administration chapter; or

- interview of a human resource specialist.

Classroom Discussion:

Have each group list its top ten items on the board. Each group should give a brief presentation discussing the pros and cons of each item. Which item(s) would be easiest to implement? Which item(s) would be the least expensive to implement? Which item(s) would be most appreciated by employees?

IN-SERVICE STUDENTS

Part I—Classification

Instructions:

Form groups of three to five members. Each group should select one public sector organization, then contact the classification specialist in that organization's human resource department. Interview the specialist to determine

- which classification system (e.g., point-factor system, position classification, broadbanding) the organization uses;
- what the advantages and disadvantages are of using the system;
- whether the specialist likes using the current system;
- how well department heads, supervisors, and employees understand and respond to the system;
- whether the human resource department conducts training sessions on the classification system for managers and employees; and
- whether there are any other issues regarding the organization's classification system.

Collect a sample of a position description and the classification specification/standard to which the position belongs. Look at the fit between the position description and classification specification/standard from the perspective of a department manager or employee to determine whether the position appears to fit well with the specification/standard. In class, each group should report on their findings from the interviews and examination of the samples. Discuss the insights gained from viewing the process in several public sector organizations.

Part 2—Nonmonetary Rewards

Instructions:

Have each student use the nonmonetary rewards that were identified in this chapter along with others added by the class to survey ten employees and their supervisors in a public sector organization. Ask the employees to rank from one (the highest) to ten (the lowest) the factors that *they most want* from their jobs. Ask the supervisors to rank from one to ten the factors that *they think* the employees most want from their jobs. Bring the results to a class meeting designated by the instructor.

Workshop Project

Working in groups of approximately five, have students compare their results and identify patterns and trends. Have each group select a spokesperson to report the findings to the class. Then analyze the results across groups. What advice would the class give to public sector employers concerning reward systems based on their findings?

NOTES

1. Joan E. Pynes, *Human Resources Management*, 73.

2. Published government reports, management studies, and other documents are routinely deposited in special government document libraries throughout the United States. These libraries are usually located at land-grant colleges in each state. Government documents are organized by the originating federal department, such as Labor, Commerce, or Health and Human Services.

3. Stahl, *Public Personnel Administration*, 184.

4. *HR Explanation and Advice* (New York: Research Institute of America Group, 1997), 2.

5. Sandra L. O'Neil, "Broadbanding," in Society for Human Resource Management [database online] (Alexandria, VA: SHRM, 2 September 1997 [cited 8 March 2000]), member-restricted access at http://www.shrm.org/docs/whitepapers/wp4.html.

6. "History of Broadbanding," *Broadbanding: Volume III*, in IPMA [database online] (Alexandria, VA: IPMA [cited 8 March 2000]), member-restricted access at http://www.ipma-hr.org.

7. Ibid.

8. "Broadbanding in the Public Sector," *Broadbanding: Volume III*, in IPMA [database online] (Alexandria, VA: IPMA [cited 8 March 2000]), member-restricted access at http://www.ipma-hr.org.

9. "Placing Positions into Bands," *Broadbanding: Volume III*, in IPMA [database online] (Alexandria, VA: IPMA [cited 8 March 2000]), member-restricted access at http://www.ipma-hr.org.

10. "Strengths and Weaknesses of Broadbanding Systems," *Broadbanding: Volume III*, in IPMA ([database online] Alexandria, VA: IPMA [cited 8 March 2000]), member-restricted access at http://www.ipma-hr.org.

11. "Pay for Performance: Focus on Organizational and Individual Performance," *IPMA CPR Series: Pay for Performance*, in IPMA [database online] (Alexandria, VA: IPMA [cited 7 March 2000]), member-restricted access at http://www.ipma-hr.org.

12. Ibid.

13. James L. Perry, "Compensation, Merit Pay and Motivation," in *Public Personnel Administration: Problems and Prospects*, eds. Steven Hays and Richard C. Kearney (Englewood Cliffs, NJ: Prentice Hall, 1995), 122.

14. "Gainsharing," *IPMA CPR Series*, in IPMA [database online] (Alexandria, VA: IPMA [cited 8 March 2000]), member-restricted access at http://www.ipma-hr.org.

15. Ibid.

16. "Employee Recognition & Rewards II," *CPR Series*, in IPMA [database online] (Alexandria, VA: IPMA, March 1999 [cited 8 March 2000]), member-restricted access at http://www.ipma-hr.org.

MEETING DEPARTMENTAL GOALS: PERFORMANCE ASSESSMENT

THE VALUE OF PERFORMANCE APPRAISALS

If used appropriately, performance appraisal or performance evaluation is a tool that helps keep the overall unit moving toward obtaining the desired outcomes of the organization and facilitates employee success on the job. It can be a powerful component of manager-employee planning, assessment, and goal attainment. An effective performance appraisal system will provide information to managers about whether employees are working toward the established mission in an acceptable manner at the required level of effort. Feedback from a performance appraisal can help reinforce a worker's performance, bring about performance improvement, and identify needed areas of training. Documenting performance can also provide managers with a sound basis for making decisions about retention, promotion, merit raises, layoffs, discipline, and termination.

Admittedly, performance appraisal systems are often viewed negatively by both employees and managers. Evaluation time can be stressful for employees, especially when the performance appraisal system allows for too much subjectivity. All too often, workers sense that the evaluation does not adequately measure performance, and they wonder if performance and reward are truly linked. At the same time, managers do not like dealing with workers who get easily upset at evaluation time, who threaten to file grievances and lawsuits, or who sabotage the work environment because they are angry.

Both the department head and the human resource department have the responsibility to establish a quality performance appraisal system that measures actual performance, treats all workers fairly and equally, eliminates rater bias and subjectivity, connects performance with suitable outcomes, and promotes the best interests of both workers and managers. Unfortunately, lack of planning, unclear expectations, ambiguous standards, and concerns for a performance appraisal system that is easy to administer frequently result in an evaluation system that is invalid and unreliable.

Typically, managers must use an inadequate appraisal form that requires them to check a series of descriptors such as excellent, good, average, or poor (i.e., the forced choice method) to evaluate generic job factors (such as quantity and quality of work) or personal characteristics (such as personality, appearance, temperament, and loyalty) that can apply to any position from tree trimmer to budget analyst. But what does this really tell the employee? How did the employee's performance contribute to the advancement or productivity of the unit? How did the performance contribute to his or her own professional development or the development of the unit? Do these appraisal methods provide adequate indicators of what the employee needs to do to improve, or does the method used require the manager to draw conclusions that may not appear to emerge naturally from the content of the appraisal itself?

Luthy addressed several of these questions. He stated:

> Work over the past two decades has consistently indicated that individual contributions must be based on clear direction, personal planning, individual and team assignments, and well-articulated knowledge, skills and personal attributes. Without such clarity, employees have no expectations to meet; nor are they able to follow patterns that constitute standard performance ideals in the organization. Only when time is taken to develop a job model for each employee, with detailed assignments and an opportunity for peer review, will evaluation be worthwhile and provide a sensible basis for personal and professional development, career advancement, and merit compensation.[1]

Since many performance appraisal methods do not adequately deal with these issues, the process is sometimes viewed as relatively meaningless and clearly to be avoided. This chapter reviews some of the major problems associated with performance appraisals and describes several contemporary approaches being used to produce more effective and valuable evaluation programs.

ISSUES CONFRONTING MANAGERS AND EMPLOYEES

Since measuring public service activities is less concrete than evaluating sales or production levels, public sector managers have had difficulty finding effective ways to verify performance and document accomplishments or improvements within their units. Major issues involved in effectively using performance appraisals include legal requirements, subjectivity, specificity, productivity, accountability, individual merit, value to the employee, time factor for the manager, and effective methodologies or approaches.

LEGAL REQUIREMENTS

Several acts, such as Title VII of the Civil Rights Act of 1964, the Age Discrimination in Employment Act of 1967, and the Americans with Disabilities Act of 1990, currently protect employees from discrimination in the workplace. This includes discrimination that may occur as a result of conducting a performance appraisal. The Uniform Guidelines on Employee Selection Procedures were issued in order to implement the provisions of Title VII. Under these guidelines, performance appraisals are regarded as a selection procedure when used to make decisions concerning an individual's employment status.[2] Therefore, they must meet the same requirements as any other test under the guidelines and must be supported by information gathered in a job analysis. As indicated in Chapter 3, even if affirmative action does not remain lawful for most public agencies, the underlying premise of these laws reinforces merit principles concerning the use of exclusively job-related standards of fitness for the position.

Performance appraisals must not have adverse impact under current law, that is, they cannot disproportionately screen out protected classes, such as minorities and women; and their content must demonstrate job relatedness. For managers this means that decisions based on performance appraisals concerning dismissal or release from probation, nonpromotion, demotion, and denial of merit pay cannot be based on subjective criteria, or the human resource action will be challenged in court. As indicated in the Uniform Guidelines, a thorough job analysis helps define job-related performance standards. With objective knowledge about work expectations, it is easier to establish a standardized performance appraisal system that rates actual performance instead of subjective traits.

Eliminating the use of performance appraisals will not circumvent these legal issues. Without formal appraisals, managers are left with no written, job-related documentation to justify their actions and decisions. Thus, they would be even more vulnerable to grievances and legal actions.

SUBJECTIVITY

Employees frequently complain that their supervisor's evaluation of their performance is too subjective, either because the evaluation criteria are too subjective or the evaluator is biased. Appraisals often contain subjective factors such as motivation, integrity, or commitment. There is little doubt that managers want and need motivated employees, but how can they measure, evaluate, and improve an employee's motivation? If a manager indicates that an employee's motivation to perform the job needs improvement, very often the employee will respond with "What do you mean?" in order to demonstrate to the manager that he or she has no idea what constitutes adequate motivation. Alternatively, some employees may be more confrontational and state, "But I *am* motivated!" as a technique to put the evaluator on the defense and force the inquisitor to prove inadequate motivation. Using subjective factors in the performance appraisal process often makes employees feel that they are being personally attacked. Thus, the most natural human response is to become defensive.

Translating subjective factors into more objective (i.e., job-based) factors provides a means for shifting the focus from personal attack to job goals

TABLE 4-1	TRANSLATING SUBJECTIVE FACTORS INTO JOB-BASED FACTORS
Subjective Factors	**Job-Based Factors**
Motivation to perform the job	Completes projects or assignments on or before the deadline Completes projects or assignments independently Obtains data or information to support and enhance projects
Integrity	Follows through with concrete results or responses on job-related commitments made to staff members, colleagues, and supervisors Does not violate conflict-of-interest policy Consistently follows through on promises made concerning job-related matters Follows organization's code of ethics
Ability to get along with others	Successfully completes projects or assignments that require information, involvement, and/or cooperation with peers Uses his/her job knowledge to help others while maintaining his/her own workload Responds quickly to questions or requests for information from peers and managers

or needs. In the case of subjective factors, this would require starting with these factors and translating them into criteria that more clearly describe job expectations. It may require multiple descriptors for one subjective factor, since a factor like motivation really affects several areas of job performance. Table 4-1 provides several examples of translating subjective factors into job-based criteria.

This process requires considerable thought because managers themselves may not know what they mean or want when they insist on these personal characteristics.

Table 4-2 summarizes the problems encountered by using subjective factors and the benefits derived from converting these to job-based factors.

Even with objective, job-related evaluation criteria, workers may still be skeptical about the fairness of a performance appraisal system because the rater may apply the criteria in a subjective manner. Rater bias is common and attempts to deal with it should be made on an ongoing basis.

Rater bias may take several different forms. The "halo effect" occurs when a rater allows one positive factor or characteristic to influence other ratings. For example, the rater believes that loyalty is the most important characteristic of a good employee. The employee being rated is very loyal; therefore, the rater assumes that the employee must also be outstanding in the quantity and quality of work produced. The "rusty halo effect" is the exact opposite. The rater allows one negative rating factor to become the employee's rating in all other areas, regardless of the actual performance. Workers are very aware of the halo and rusty halo effects. Thus, it is not unusual to find workers putting

TABLE 4-2	USING SUBJECTIVE VERSUS JOB-BASED FACTORS
Problems Encountered Using Subjective Factors	**Benefits Gained Using Job-Based Factors**
Managers may be forced into a defensive posture	Identification and provision of more concrete information for the purpose of evaluation
Unclear descriptions of expected employee behaviors may result	Identification of specific behaviors expected from the employee
Problem solving may be impeded	Identification of job-related factors that can facilitate problem solving
Defensive employee responses may result	Identification of specific work-related needs, goals, and results, minimizing the importance of personal characteristics
Clear goals and expectations may not be provided	Identification in writing of goals and expectations

in extra effort, arriving early for work, and staying longer hours while avoiding mistakes, not taking any risks, and so forth, just before the performance evaluation is due.

Some raters are unable or unwilling to rate the employee accurately or fairly on each evaluation factor. The "central tendency error" occurs when the evaluator slants the employee's evaluation so that the overall outcome is average. The "leniency error" and "severity error" are similar. In the former, the tendency is to give high ratings, and in the latter, to give ratings that are lower. While giving all employees favorable evaluations may keep them from getting upset in the short term, the long-term effects can be devastating. Workers will eventually lose trust in the evaluation system and their managers. Workers who are really top performers will feel that they are not being properly rewarded for their efforts since ineffective workers are also getting rewarded for not putting in much effort. The good workers will leave and the workers with the inaccurate view of themselves will stay. Now when the manager attempts to deal with the less-than-effective workers, the discredited evaluation system will not support disciplinary action, especially when the workers' personnel records contain years of satisfactory performance evaluations.

SPECIFICITY, PRODUCTIVITY, AND ACCOUNTABILITY

Unclear or unexpressed expectations create another performance appraisal problem. Employees often argue that managers evaluate them using standards or criteria that they were not aware of prior to receiving their performance appraisal. Managers often mistakenly believe that employees already know what is expected of them, but managers may not clearly express what they expect. They may fail to follow up to see if these expectations were understood, or they may neglect to provide regular performance feedback outside of the formal performance appraisal system.

Problems concerning performance expectations often lead to unacceptable levels of productivity and confusion about accountability. For example, if a manager in the parks and recreation department asked an employee to check the gas in a truck that is transporting new recreation equipment, is the employee's job only to see how much gas is in the truck? Or was the employee also expected to fill the gas tank, check the engine compartment fluid levels, make sure the equipment is secured, and warm up the truck? If the employee does not do all of these things, and the supervisor fails to tell him or her what meets or falls below the expectations, how will the employee know what to do the next time?

Dealing with such problems requires the development of written performance standards that can be measured or observed by the evaluator. The development and discussion of these standards with employees through a thorough job analysis (see Chapter 3) can serve to reduce confusion about what managers expect and what results employees must obtain, thereby establishing increased clarity and accountability.

Personnel specialists can develop and describe performance standards in a manner that will allow evaluators to observe the outcomes. An outcome may be in the form of reports, case summaries, implementation of programs or services, increases or decreases in services, or completion of tasks. The fact that government is service-based and not involved in sales or production does not mean that outcomes should not and cannot be evaluated and accountability established.

INDIVIDUAL MERIT

Managers generally want to recognize and reward employees who demonstrate outstanding performance. Recognition of outstanding performance lets employees know that their efforts have significant value to the organization. It sets an example and provides incentives for other employees. It indicates to employees that performance really matters.

Paradoxically, however, recognizing and rewarding individual merit is one of the most frustrating aspects of performance appraisal for both managers and employees. When subjective evaluation criteria are used, it is difficult to identify superior performance and distinguish it from personal preferences. Without specific performance objectives and standards, managers have a difficult time explaining why certain employees earned high evaluations and why the performance of others does not merit high ratings and accompanying increases in pay. Employees have a difficult time with performance appraisal systems if there is little connection between their work efforts, the performance evaluation rating, and merit pay.

Merit pay and pay-for-performance systems are not without controversy and difficulties in administration. The Civil Service Reform Act of 1978 included provisions for federal supervisors, managers, and Senior Executive Service (SES) employees to receive merit pay or bonuses for superior performance based on goal-oriented appraisal systems. Unfortunately for early SES participants, Congress initially failed to allocate sufficient funds to pay these bonuses and the amount of these bonuses was controversial. Currently, SES employees may be nominated for and receive Presidential Rank Awards for outstanding performance.

Various state, local, and county governments, and school districts throughout the country also have merit pay systems. In some cases, adequate funds have not been made available to implement the program. In the city of La Mesa (CA), for example, uniformed staff were allowed to have a merit bonus, but the bonus was contained within a single budgetary year and did not add to their base pay. By paying out the bonus over the entire year, however, the city did not realize that some employees were living beyond their means. When the new budget year started, the uniformed staff thought that their pay had been reduced.

In other cases, merit plans are difficult to administer because they are tied to poorly constructed or poorly administered performance appraisal instruments. Still another problem is the human difficulty of dealing with the employee's disappointment or anger when little or no increase is granted. Though there are methods available to reduce these problems, granting merit increases or bonuses based on evaluations of performance is a difficult challenge for public sector managers. There are no easy answers to this challenge. However, improving the evaluation tool and criteria linked to merit pay is a step in the right direction. Developing clear criteria for the distribution of merit pay and sharing them with employees is another approach. Seeking nonmonetary rewards (see Chapter 3) based on employee suggestions or preferences may also help, especially when funds are limited.

TIME-CONSUMING PROCESS

Managers often view performance appraisal as a separate function that requires considerable expenditure of time and effort apart from the primary work or function of the unit. Thus, the performance appraisal process, no matter how well developed, becomes viewed as a burden which takes time away from pressing priorities in the work unit.

THE DEPARTMENT MANAGER'S ROLE IN PERFORMANCE APPRAISAL

The department manager plays the most critical role in the performance appraisal process. Other than the employee, the manager or immediate supervisor is the primary person who can fully assess the employee's actual job performance. The human resource department is responsible for the

TABLE 4-3 RESPONSIBILITY FOR PERFORMANCE APPRAISAL	
Human Resource Department	**Department Manager**
Develops appropriate performance appraisal method and forms with input from department manager	Provides input to human resource department on performance appraisal needs and/or implementation problems at the department level
Provides a position description to each employee	Discusses job duties, performance standards, and expectations with the employee
Notifies manager of due dates for completed performance appraisal for employee under his/her supervision; monitors completion and return of forms	Administers performance appraisal process within the department: ■ communicates performance expectations and requirements to employee ■ observes/assesses employee's work ■ completes appraisal form/tool ■ reviews appraisal with employee ■ establishes standards and expectations for the next evaluation period ■ informs human resource department of effectiveness or ineffectiveness of the appraisal method when necessary

development of the performance appraisal method but does not assess the employee's performance.

For this process to be effective, department managers need to receive training in implementing the performance appraisal process, emphasizing the human dimension and the appraisal method. In addition, the human resource department has to be aware of the department manager's assessment of the strengths and weaknesses of the performance appraisal method being used for positions in his/her department. Is it feasible to use the same method to evaluate police officers, accountants, and secretaries? If not, what method would work best for each of these categories? Table 4-3 outlines the responsibilities of the human resource department and department manager in the performance appraisal process.

CONTEMPORARY PERFORMANCE APPRAISAL METHODS

In order to overcome many of the problems identified above, some organizations have moved away from traditional forced choice methods with generic descriptors to more competency-based methods such as goal setting, critical incidence, behaviorally anchored rating scales, performance planning, and

360-degree evaluations. Competency-based appraisals allow managers to evaluate authentic job performance rather than personality, and consequently, managers are able to hold employees accountable to all stakeholders, including public sector clients and the community. Below, Luthy describes a process that fits the meaning of competency-based performance appraisals.

> Perhaps most important here is a new process that removes much of the subjectivity from performance evaluation and replaces it with objectives and actions required by the job, as defined in advance by both supervisor and employee. Removing the subjective aspect of employee evaluations is in itself a major advance from most systems being used today.[3]

GOAL SETTING

Using the goal-setting method of performance appraisal, the manager and employee work jointly to develop specific goals to be accomplished for the employee's position during an identified period of time (e.g., one year). Performance standards are identified for each goal that describe the expected level of performance to satisfactorily meet the goal. Once the goals and standards are established, the employee completes the work and the manager records the results of his or her performance. The results are then evaluated against the previously established standards and rated to determine whether the employee's performance met, exceeded, or fell below the standard. A written assessment of the employee's performance in each goal area is provided to specifically describe how well the goal was met or whether improvement or training is needed. The manager and employee meet to discuss the appraisal, identify improvements, if any, and set new goals and standards for the next evaluation period. Table 4-4 provides an example of the goal-setting performance appraisal format.

Research on goal setting suggests that this approach has a positive motivational impact on employees in studies where a single goal was examined. The evidence is less convincing, however, in studies where multiple goals were assessed.[4] Based on this finding, Yearta, Maitlis, and Briner propose that the periods between goal setting should be considerably reduced and that the appraiser's involvement increased to maximize the benefits of this method.[5] Acknowledging these cautions, the goal-setting method offers a number of advantages over traditional methods and some disadvantages for managers and employees (see Table 4-5).

CRITICAL INCIDENCE

The critical incidence method involves periodic observations of the performance behaviors of the employee by the manager. This method includes a definition of the duties to be performed or goals to be attained, identification of acceptable standards of performance, and mutual involvement of the employee and manager.[6] There are specified observation periods during the

| TABLE 4-4 | GOAL-SETTING PERFORMANCE APPRAISAL FORMAT |

Position Title: Appointment Documents Clerk

Duties of Position	Goals	Performance Standard(s)	Time Frame for Completion	Performance Results	Evaluation of Results	Rating (E,M,I,D)
Process appointment documents to hire part-time employees	Complete paperwork to hire 200 part-time employees by August 1	Prepare and mail employment contracts for 200 employees with correct information regarding salary, time base, beginning and ending dates	June 15–August 1	Employee completed all 200 contracts by August 1. Errors were reported in 5% of the contracts.	Output and completion date met the required standards. However, employee needs to work on errors in salary and appointment fraction calculations.	M = output I = accuracy

Comments: Because this employee is new to the position, the supervisor will need to provide additional training to the employee during the next rating period. Rating Scale: E = Exceeds standards; I = Improvement needed in specific areas; M = Meets standards; D = Does not meet standards

TABLE 4-5	ADVANTAGES AND DISADVANTAGES OF GOAL SETTING

Advantages	Disadvantages
Goal setting involves both employees and managers, which allows for mutual discussion, clarification and problem solving	Process is time-consuming for managers and employees
Goal setting focuses on the employee's performance or the impact of the employee's performance on the unit, thus reducing the impact of subjective or non-job-related factors	Specific performance standards are not simple to develop and measure for public service positions.
	Process may not be appropriate or provide maximum effectiveness for all public service positions.
Employees and managers know what performance is expected during the evaluation period, thereby providing more accountability in the process.	Evaluation period may be too long to allow for corrections and appropriate prioritizing.
Employees can assess the results of their performance even before the manager's appraisal, using the expectations and standards identified before the evaluation period begins.	Does not provide an easy method of comparison among positions.
	Goal setting does not work if worker cannot control work processes that lead to goal achievement
Surprises, confrontations, and conflicts should be reduced.	

appraisal process when the manager observes the employee's performance or output using the established criteria. A sample of the critical incidence method is included in Table 4-6.

The critical incidence appraisal system is often used effectively for positions where the work behaviors are readily observable and the work is performed away from the manager or supervisor, such as bus driver or recreation leader. The key to success is adequately sampling the work activities throughout the evaluation period. Failure to do so will affect the fairness of the evaluation. Table 4-7 lists the advantages and disadvantages of this appraisal method.

BEHAVIORALLY ANCHORED RATING SCALE (BARS)

Behaviorally anchored rating scale (BARS) is an appraisal method that links descriptions of the possible performance that an employee might exhibit to a numbered rating scale for each duty (see Table 4-8). It is a more detailed version of the critical incidence appraisal method.[7] The rating scales are developed through joint collaboration among human resource specialists, employees who perform the duties, and the manager or supervisor. The most important or critical duties of the position are identified using job analysis.

TABLE 4-6 CRITICAL INCIDENCE PERFORMANCE APPRAISAL FORMAT

Position Title: Recreation Coordinator

Duties of Position	Performance Standards	Number of Observations during Rating Period	Observed Performance	Evaluation of Results	Rating (E,M,I,D)
Plan, organize, and coordinate activities for the city's Department of Recreation	Plan and implement "Concert in the Park" series. Concert 1: The Calypso Steel Band ■ Schedule band and process band's contract three months prior to concert ■ Release publicity one month prior to performance ■ Arrange for equipment and setup three weeks prior to concert ■ Supervise the event on the day of the concert	3 observations. Supervisor will review completed paperwork and publicity releases, and will observe event on the scheduled day.	Band was scheduled and contract was processed three months prior to concert. Publicity was released three weeks prior to the event. Equipment and setup arranged one month prior to concert. Event was fully supervised.	Band was scheduled on time; setup was scheduled early. All paperwork was filed correctly. Publicity was released one week late which could have contributed to slightly lower attendance. Event was properly supervised.	M = Event scheduling E = Paperwork completion I = Publicity M = Event supervision

Rating Scale: E = Exceeds standards; I = Improvement needed in specific areas; M = Meets standards; D = Does not meet standards.

TABLE 4-7	ADVANTAGES AND DISADVANTAGES OF CRITICAL INCIDENCE PERFORMANCE APPRAISAL

Advantages	Disadvantages
Works well for positions where primary performance factors are readily observable	Does not work if employee cannot control work processes that lead to successful performance
Appropriate for positions where the supervisor is not present continually	Observations are time-consuming for managers
Appraisal is developed based on essential duties of the position	Appraisal form has to be redeveloped when major evaluation factors change
Employees and managers know what performance is expected during the evaluation period	Evaluation period may be too long to allow for corrections and appropriate prioritizing

TABLE 4-8	BEHAVIORALLY ANCHORED RATING SCALE FORMAT

Position: Receptionist

Performance Factor: Providing Information to the Public

4 = Greets visitor immediately; takes time to fully understand visitor's need for information; refers visitor to appropriate department/individual; if uncertain about referral, calls department/individual prior to visitor leaving reception area to assure that visitor is being properly directed

3 = Greets visitor; answers questions asked by visitor and provides additional direction if needed

2 = Recognizes presence of visitor, but provides only minimal information

1 = Does not recognize presence of visitor until individual gains attention from employee; becomes annoyed if visitor is too persistent

For each duty the group develops a series of descriptors that identify a range of performance from the least desirable to the most desirable. The descriptors are numbered from highest to lowest rank or rating. When employees begin their position, they are given a copy of the evaluation form to acquaint them with the performance expectations of the position. The manager observes the employee's performance, then circles the number of the behavior that best describes the employee's performance.

This appraisal process has a number of advantages, as well as disadvantages, over traditional forced choice methods with generic descriptors (see Table 4-9). BARS is especially effective for job classifications with large

TABLE 4-9	ADVANTAGES AND DISADVANTAGES OF BARS
Advantages	**Disadvantages**
Process is individually designed for each job classification, thus does not include problems inherent in generic descriptors	Initial process is detailed and time-consuming to develop
Appraisal is developed with involvement of employees who perform duties of the position	Appraisal form has to be redeveloped when major evaluation factors change
Evaluation is simple to administer and re-quires relatively little time in comparison to other methods	Method is not appropriate or effective for all public sector positions
Employees are provided clear, written de-scriptions of performance expectations in advance of evaluation period	May not emphasize teamwork unless teamwork is a performance expectation
Process helps reduce surprises for em-ployees and confrontations or conflicts with the manager	

numbers of employees that have essentially similar roles, responsibilities, duties, and expectations.

PERFORMANCE PLANNING

Several leading-edge organizations have titled their performance appraisal tool "performance planning." Since performance planning extends far beyond the instrument itself, this process requires a shift in focus that is forward-looking and dynamic while integrating performance appraisal into its natural context—the overall planning and functioning of the unit.[8] Performance planning is quite viable in the public sector though this approach is most often used by private sector organizations at the present time.[9] It requires managers and employees to focus on the priorities of the unit, the output or work to be accomplished during a certain period of time, the resources available, and the individuals or work teams that will accomplish each identified priority. In addition to this basic planning approach, the process requires the involvement of each member of the unit from clerical employees to managers. Unit members meet, develop the plan, identify each participant's role, and have each participant prepare a written planning sheet (see Table 4-10) outlining his/her role and responsibilities during specific time periods. Then the manager distributes all planning sheets to each member of the unit. Scheduled meetings are held to discuss progress, to reestablish or redefine priorities, to seek suggestions from team members, and to distribute updated planning sheets.

This process is ongoing, responsive to changing priorities, and mutually supportive. Inherent in the process is performance feedback. Unit members are provided with ongoing appraisal of their projects and progress. The manager and unit members are aware of each other's progress and receive feedback from group members. As a natural outcome of performance planning and not as a separate process, unit member's planning sheets and outcomes documenting the progress of each member provide the data for the formal appraisal. The advantages and disadvantages of this process are outlined in Table 4-11.

Often, one major benefit of this approach is the outcome produced by the process itself. The structure of the performance planning process allows an opportunity for group problem solving and interaction. As each group member describes his or her projects, goals, and potential problems, other members often recommend approaches, resources, and solutions that may help facilitate successful completion of the project or goals. This dynamic helps to further the development of a unit as a more cohesive team, and thus furthers the goals of the individual employee, the unit, and the organization.

360-Degree Evaluation

Another performance appraisal method that has gained favor in recent years is the 360-degree evaluation. In this appraisal method, employees receive feedback on their performance from peers, those whom the employee supervises, service recipients/customers, and the employee's immediate manager. The employee also has an opportunity to perform a self-evaluation. A 360-degree evaluation can be used as the sole performance appraisal approach or in conjunction with the performance planning method to provide feedback for professional and interpersonal development.[10]

The evaluation includes a major focus on interpersonal skills that highlight the individual's ability to work well with others in order to accomplish the goals of his or her job. Most often, managers and executives receive 360-degree evaluations to provide insight about their performance from several perspectives and to assist in the employee's professional and personal development. The Center for Creative Leadership, for example, provides managers and executives with 360-degree evaluations during their leadership training. Obviously, this method must be explained properly to the evaluators and designed carefully to promote fairness and constructive feedback. Table 4-12 summarizes several advantages and disadvantages of the 360-degree evaluation method.

| TABLE 4-10 | PERFORMANCE PLANNING RATING FORMAT/PLANNING SHEET |

Position Title: Program Coordinator

Part I — Planning

Organization Goals	Department/ Unit Goals	Specific Employee Goals and/or Activities	Resources Needed	Potential Problems/ Frustrations	Overall Time Frame for Completing Goals and/or Activities	Interim Assessment Period (if applicable)
Increase the use of computers to enhance communication between field offices and the central office	Provide each of the three supervisors in Region B with a computer, printer, and software	Prepare budget request for purchase of computer equipment and software Prepare purchase order for equipment and software Arrange for installation of equipment and software Arrange for training of supervisors to use equipment and software	Funding for the purchase of equipment and software	Delays in obtaining funding and receiving equipment	October 15 to February 15	By December 1, assess progress and determine whether delays or problems exist

Part II — Assessment

Standards for Assessing Results	Results/Accomplishments	Assessment of Results	Rating (E,M,I,D)
Budget request prepared and presented to program director by October 31	Submitted budget request to supervisor by October 20	Adherence to time lines met and often exceeded standards	E = Time lines, Content, Output Employee is not held responsible for one-month delay created in other offices
Within 5 work days after receiving budget approval, purchase order prepared and submitted to procurement office	Prepared and submitted purchase order within 5 work days after budget approval	Content of budget was clearly and accurately written	
Once equipment and software are received, arrange for installation within 7 work days	Arranged for installation of equipment and software within 4 work days after receipt	Paperwork for procurement was complete and accurate	
Schedule training session for supervisors within 5 work days after installation	Scheduled training within 5 days after installation of equipment	Installation and training sessions were arranged in a timely manner and met the needs of each supervisor	
Total project completed by February 15	Project completed by March 2	December 1 assessment revealed that project delays were created by individuals in other offices and were not the responsibility of the employee	

Rating Scale: E = Exceeds standards; M = Meets standards; I = Improvement needed in specific areas; D = Does not meet standards

TABLE 4-11	ADVANTAGES AND DISADVANTAGES OF PERFORMANCE PLANNING

Advantages	Disadvantages
Establishes an integrated work plan at specified intervals (i.e., annually, semiannually, quarterly)	Process is time-consuming during initial establishment and update periods
Involves every member of the work unit including managers, professional, technical, and secretarial employees	Implementing the process is more difficult for more introverted managers
Uses written planning sheets prepared and updated by each unit member	Some initial uneasiness may occur due to the nontraditional mix of employees and the openness of the process
Incorporates scheduled unit meetings to monitor progress, provide team input, and evaluate priorities	Constant need to update plan and forms
	May invite "free riders"
Includes individual meetings or updates between the manager and each unit member as needed in between group meetings	Sometimes difficult to distinguish individual effort from group effort
	Individuals may not want input from group members
Incorporates evaluation or appraisal of individual performance based on information from the total performance planning process	Union may object
Facilitates team approach, joint problem solving, and goal attainment	

TABLE 4-12	ADVANTAGES AND DISADVANTAGES OF THE 360-DEGREE EVALUATION METHOD

Advantages	Disadvantages
Reduces subjectivity associated with evaluations conducted solely by the supervisor[a]	Ratings inconsistent due to employee's roles and relationships with different constituencies[b]
Provides feedback from evaluators who are in the best position to rate the employee's performance	Raises uncertainty about whether the evaluation should be used for development only or evaluation[c]
Facilitates more accurate evaluation of the employee's off-site or independent performance	Individual may not be ready to accept the feedback and make needed changes[d]
Provides an effective tool for the employee's professional and personal development	Increases direct and indirect cost to the organization for preparation and implementation[e]
Helps the individual better understand the impact of his/her management style on employees[f]	May cause role conflict if employee has different expectations from different people or constituents[g]
	May be biased by personal retribution from coworkers or professional jealousy

[a] James Fox and Charles Klein, "The 360-Degree Evaluation," *Public Management* 78 (November 1996): 20.
[b] Walter W. Tornow, Manuel London, and CCL Associates, "The Challenges and Implications for Maximizing 360-Degree Feedback," in *Maximizing the Value of 360-Degree Feedback: A Process for Successful Individual and Organizational Development* (San Francisco: Jossey-Bass, 1998), 250.
[c] Ibid., 252.　[d] Ibid., 250.　[e] Ibid., 251.　[f] Ibid.　[g] Ibid., 252.

WORKSHOP 4

Performance Assessment

PRE-SERVICE STUDENTS

Developing Performance Factors

"Quality of Work" and "Quantity of Work" are two subjective performance factors that often appear on performance appraisal forms. The goal of this exercise is to turn these factors into objective performance appraisal tools.

Format:

Pick a job classification on campus or in a public sector organization, such as human resource analyst, department manager, secretary, or budget analyst. Have the class discuss what job-based factors are indicators of "quality" and "quantity" of work.

Break the class into three groups:

- Group One will write a performance appraisal system that is based on the goal-setting method.
- Group Two will use the critical incidence method.
- Group Three will establish a BARS system.

Group Discussion:

- How are the performance appraisal systems similar? How do they differ?
- Describe some of the difficulties encountered in defining the appraisal factors using the various appraisal systems.
- Which performance appraisal system would most appeal to workers?
- Which of the methods is easiest to administer? What could be done to improve ease of administration?

Analyzing Performance Appraisal Forms

There are a variety of criteria and formats used to evaluate performance. The purpose of this exercise is to analyze the variety of approaches, classify them, and discuss methods for improving them.

Instructions:

Assign students the task of gathering performance appraisal forms from a variety of public and private sector organizations. Employed students may use their current performance appraisal form (with personal information blocked out). Unemployed students may wish to approach a roommate or parent, go to a government documents library, or inquire at a local personnel office. Each student should bring five copies of the evaluation form to class.

Divide the class into groups of five students. Instruct students to classify the performance appraisal forms by major type (goal setting, critical incidence, etc.), rate the forms in terms of subjectivity versus objectivity, and rate the forms by ease of administration. Then rank order the forms.

Each group then passes its collection of forms on to another group for an independent assessment.

Classroom Discussion:

Each group reports on its original set of performance appraisal forms. What were the top ranking forms? Why were they rated highly? Do the other groups concur?

After all groups have presented and critiqued the evaluation forms, what is the class consensus about an adequate performance appraisal form?

IN-SERVICE STUDENTS

Instructions:

Form groups of approximately five members. Have each employed group member briefly describe his or her position. Select one member's position in each group as a focus for this workshop. Alternatively, the group can arrange to bring an individual on the day of the workshop whose job would be of interest to the group.

Workshop Project

Have the selected individual describe three to five of his or her most important job duties. Based on the nature of the position and duties:

- Determine which of the performance appraisal methods described in this chapter would be most appropriate to evaluate this position. Provide a rationale for this choice. Consider such factors as

  - can the supervisor readily observe the employee's performance or end product, or will the supervisor have to set up specific observation times and locations;

  - is the job performed by a substantial number of individuals who do very similar tasks under similar circumstances; and

  - do the assignments vary substantially for different individuals in the same classification?

- After considering these factors, review the strengths and weaknesses of each performance appraisal method to help determine the approach that appears best for evaluation of the selected position.

- Using the selected appraisal method, develop a sample performance appraisal based on the three to five duties described earlier. This will require in-depth questioning of the interviewee to determine such factors as

- what output, service, or activity would the supervisor observe or measure to determine that each duty is being performed; and
- what is the acceptable level of output or outcome for each duty?
- Based on this information, develop performance standards and rating criteria.

NOTES

1. John Luthy, "New Keys to Employee Performance and Productivity," *Public Management* 80 (March 1998): 4.

2. U.S. EEOC, "Uniform Guidelines." See also, Andrew L. Klein, "Validity and Reliability for Competency-Based Systems: Reducing the Litigation Risks," *Compensation and Benefits Review* 28 (July–August 1996): 32.

3. Luthy, "New Keys," 6.

4. Shawn K. Yearta, Sally Maitlis, and Rob B. Briner, "An Exploratory Study of Goal Setting in Theory and Practice: A Motivational Technique That Works?" *Journal of Occupational and Organizational Psychology* 68 (September 1995): 251.

5. Ibid.

6. Robert L. Cardy, "Performance Appraisal in a Quality Context: A New Look at an Old Problem," in *Performance Appraisal: State of the Art in Practice,* ed. James W. Smither (San Francisco: Jossey-Bass, 1998), 150.

7. Ibid.

8. Michael G. Winston, "Leadership of Renewal: Leadership for the Twenty-first Century," *Business Forum* 22 (winter 1997): 6.

9. One of the coauthors used this method successfully in a public sector organization.

10. Ibid.

5

Managing Performance Improvement

Managing today's employees is particularly complex due to the proliferation of issues that are inherent in our current society and workforce. (See chapter 8 for further discussion of managing today's employees.) Therefore, in the words of Edgar H. Schein, "The successful manager must be a good diagnostician and must value a spirit of inquiry."[1] In addition to being a diagnostician, the manager must know the characteristics, style, and work patterns of each employee, determine which problem-solving approach or combination of approaches may be effective, and understand the organizational and legal responsibilities associated with handling problem behavior.

When working with employees who are performing below expectations, the manager's goal is to find the underlying cause of the unsatisfactory performance and to provide appropriate information, tools, resources, and opportunities so that employees can become effective and productive again. Douglas McGregor's sage advice is still relevant for today's managers. We should assume that employees are intrinsically motivated to perform well on the job and they are personally dissatisfied with working below standard performance levels.[2] Adopting this philosophy generates a relationship of mutual trust and respect between managers and employees. If, on the other hand, managers assume a more traditional view of workers and believe that they are lazy, selfish, ignorant, and deliberately insubordinate, then the manager's approach will be harsh, punitive, and judgmental. The latter philosophy is likely to result in a defensive and angry worker whose focus will shift from improving work performance to getting even with the manager. The costs to the organization of such a negative approach are high. Confrontations between managers and disgruntled employees easily spill over into the workplace and lower the morale and productivity of other workers. When no common ground can be achieved, the organization not only loses the employee, but also loses the time, energy, and resources invested in that employee. Attempting to replace the "troublesome" employee with a new employee not only doubles the cost of training and development (once for the incumbent and again for the replacement), but also gives other workers the impression that managers are unwilling to work through issues with employees.

Since the working relationships in a unit are interdependent, each member's contribution is of vital importance. When one employee is unable to perform at normal levels, for whatever reason, several problems may occur:

other employees are required to assume additional duties and responsibilities; error rates, accidents, and stress-related leave requests increase; the employee neglects his or her duties resulting in a reduction in overall productivity; department morale plummets. A common human tendency is to ignore the problem and hope it disappears. If allowed to continue, however, the problem becomes exacerbated and does irreparable damage to the effectiveness of the manager and unit.

There are many reasons why worker performance may not meet expectations. The following discussion looks at several different issues: performance problems, policy compliance, job-related problems, personal problems, and ethical conduct. As Table 5-1 indicates, both manager and employee share responsibility for improving performance and job-related behaviors. The items identified under each category are intended to be illustrative rather than comprehensive. The issues in Table 5-1 are explained in the remainder of this chapter.

PERFORMANCE PROBLEMS

Problems involving employee performance generally relate to insufficient levels of productivity, preparation, skill development, compliance, or cooperation. The traditional managers' view of these problems was to assume that the workers were at fault. Thus, the customary way for managers to deal with such employees was to (1) train them so the skill deficiency was overcome, (2) transfer them to a position where their existing skills could be better utilized, or (3) fire them. A more contemporary management approach is not to automatically assume that the worker is to blame, but to thoroughly investigate the possible reasons for unsatisfactory performance. For example, a secretary's word-processing productivity may be low because the job expectations were unclear, the equipment is out-of-date, or there are family problems interfering with concentration. The actual reason for low productivity is difficult to determine without some basic fact-finding.

As indicated in Chapter 4, a number of performance problems arise because performance standards are not always clear. Ideally, the human resource department works closely with the manager to provide the employee with tools for success, such as a complete description of the duties to be performed. The manager translates the general position description into specific goals, standards, and time lines for completion. The employee is then responsible for communicating with the manager to clarify or gain better understanding of any of these factors that are unclear or confusing. But as is typical of human nature, miscommunication can occur because managers and employees may not always say what they mean. Personnel specialists can assist the manager by maintaining up-to-date job descriptions, providing training on improving communication skills, and monitoring actual work performance against job specifications.

Often, in public sector organizations, employees feel that they do not have sufficient resources (e.g., budget, equipment, staffing) to perform the job well. It is the manager's responsibility to provide leadership in seeking and obtaining resources for adequate goal attainment. If these resources are limited or unavailable, then the manager should set realistic standards for employee performance based on actual circumstances. While the personnel department is usually not involved in resource procurement, it can still assist the manager. One important way is by providing budget training in order for managers to understand the fiscal constraints of their jobs. Additionally, because human resource managers have a larger view of the organization, they can arrange for managers facing similar issues to meet together to brainstorm solutions and share knowledge of resources. By conducting periodic organizational climate surveys, personnel specialists can also help managers to understand when work expectations become detrimental to productivity. These surveys can measure a variety of attitudes and perceptions, including morale, worker-manager relations, identifying effective rewards, and so forth.

Upon evaluation of the employee's current skills and the requirements of the position, the manager must also recognize the need for further training or skills development. This is particularly important when working with a new or recently promoted employee, an employee who has been given a change in assignment or responsibility, or one who has not used certain skills recently. In most organizations, the training department is a division or an extension of the human resource department and has the necessary tools to assess current abilities, as well as the funds and staff to provide needed training.

Once the relevant tools have been provided to employees, they are responsible for performing the duties of the position and meeting the established goals and standards in a timely fashion. If problems occur with regard to meeting performance goals, having adequate resources or training, or gaining cooperation, employees should communicate their concerns to managers in a timely manner to allow sufficient opportunity for problem solving. An "open-door" policy, authentic demonstration of concern for employees, and "management by walking around" encourage open communication between worker and manager. If the employee does not feel comfortable communicating with the manager, the personnel department can serve an important function in helping that employee understand work expectations or in bridging the perceived communication gap.

Feedback and performance assessments are critical responsibilities for the manager in order to assure goal attainment and high levels of performance, and to avert or improve substandard performance. Providing formal feedback only at the annual performance appraisal, however, may be too infrequent to be of any use. Informal feedback through regular performance updates, discussions, and individual or group meetings provides opportunities for communicating satisfaction with or concerns about performance levels. When the employee's level of performance needs improvement, the manager should schedule problem-solving sessions to clearly identify and discuss performance issues, expectations for improvement, training requirements, and

TABLE 5-1	MANAGING PERFORMANCE IMPROVEMENT	
Problems	**Manager's Responsibility**	**Employee's Responsibility**
Performance Problems Low productivity Lack of ability or preparation to perform the job Noncompliance with job assignments Lack of cooperation with coworkers	Provide a complete position description Set and communicate realistic performance goals, standards, and time lines Provide basic resources for task completion Provide training opportunities for skills development Provide timely feedback and evaluation of performance Identify and discuss consequences of unchanged behavior Employ discipline procedures — progressive discipline or positive discipline (discipline without punishment)	Understand and clarify content of position description, performance goals, standards, and time lines with the manager Perform duties, meet goals and standards, comply with time lines Identify problems immediately with the manager Request necessary resources, information, and training Work cooperatively with coworkers to complete assignments Become knowledgeable about employee rights concerning discipline procedures such as due process and grievance procedures Identify possible changes in the job or work environment to alleviate problem
Policy Compliance Absenteeism and abuse of leave time (e.g., sick leave) Chronic lateness Unapproved absences	Make policies available to employees Seek assistance from human resource department Identify and discuss reasons for problems Identify and explore solutions and alternatives such as establishment of internal office procedures, time management, and flextime Identify and discuss consequences of unchanged behavior	Request information about organizational policies Discuss issues and explore options with manager concerning problems with policy compliance Change behavior to comply with policies, requirements, or agreements reached with manager
Job-Related Problems Stress Anger or disillusionment related to the job Boredom Lack of motivation Burnout	Assess how employee's behavior impacts the job Identify and evaluate factors about the job that contribute to the problem Discuss alternative courses of action with employee such as restructuring duties, work hours, office location,	Discuss problem with supervisor or manager Seek options to resolve problem with the human resource director, Employee Assistance Program coordinator, senior manager, career counselor, and/or psychological counselor *(continued)*

TABLE 5-1	CONTINUED	

Problems	Manager's Responsibility	Employee's Responsibility
Job-Related Problems	or job assignments or functions, reassignment, new skills development or training, course work or degree completion Seek assistance from the human resource department's Employee Assistance Program	Remain open to alternatives Identify and follow constructive course of action for resolving problem
Personal Problems Drug use Alcohol abuse Family dysfunction Physical and emotional changes or illness	Identify how employee's behavior impacts the job Seek assistance from human resource department's Employee Assistance Program coordinator Identify specific areas that require improvement Discuss alternative courses of action with employee such as Employee Assistance Program, treatment programs, psychological counseling, leave of absence, and/or altered work schedule or assignments Identify and discuss consequences of unchanged behavior	Seek information from Employee Assistance Program coordinator, human resource director, and/or manager concerning options such as medical and leave provisions for treatment Seek assistance from care providers or counselors and follow constructive course of action for resolving the problem Comply with job-related requirements for improved performance and/or policy compliance
Ethical Conduct Misuse of organizational property, services, equipment, and/or resources Theft Sexual harassment Lack of integrity Falsification of time records Falsification of employment application Criminal conduct	Conduct fact-finding Seek assistance from human resource department and/or legal office Identify manager's and organization's legal responsibilities and policy requirements Identify and discuss problem or allegations with employee Identify impact of employee's behavior on the job or on other employees Identify and discuss consequences of employee's actions	Request information or clarification and comply with policies, procedures, and guidelines concerning use of organization's property, services, equipment, and/or resources Review and comply with organization's sexual harassment policy Fulfill job commitments made to coworkers

time lines. If problems persist, the employee must also be informed of the possible consequences of unchanged behavior. The personnel department can be of immense help in not only teaching the manager how to effectively communicate expectations, but also helping the employee to understand the need for improved performance. Once these discussions have been completed and the employee understands the performance requirements, he or she takes on the responsibility to meet the requested requirements. When the human resource department and managers work cooperatively, the employee receives a consistent message about work expectations as well as the way in which work performance issues will be handled.

Since many jobs are interdependent and often cross departments, working cooperatively with coworkers is a common but difficult performance problem to resolve. Employees in human resource and payroll departments, for example, must rely heavily on others for accurate and timely information. Members of project teams are jointly responsible for the outcome of an assignment. Though in some cases these problems may be based on differences in personalities, the manager's problem-solving efforts should remain focused primarily on how the job or goals are impacted and what changes in approaches, procedures, work flow, or staffing need to be implemented to improve the situation. As discussed later in this chapter, some issues require third-party intervention by consultants or organization development specialists to help resolve difficulties related to team development.

POLICY COMPLIANCE

Misconduct occurs when individuals violate organizational rules or policies. To prevent misconduct, managers and personnel specialists should make sure that employees are aware of the appropriate policies and causes for disciplinary action. The human resource department can help to sensitize staff to the boundaries of established policy. Limits to discretionary informal practices can be made clear through formal information sessions such as orientation training, informal discussions, distribution of brochures, memoranda, handbooks, and the analysis of critical incidents. Another way to prevent misconduct is for managers to establish, maintain, and improve internal office reporting and scheduling procedures so that misconduct can be identified before it becomes a major problem. For example, establishing a periodic review procedure to examine mileage claims will identify those claims that are improper or potentially fraudulent. Simply knowing that such a procedure exists is often a deterrent to those who might be tempted to exploit the organization.

In addition, by establishing a practice whereby employees will seek information or clarification concerning rules, policies, and practices before taking independent action, managers can prevent inadvertent violations of policies. "When in doubt, ask" is one such practice. If expenditures are under a set amount, no supervisory approval is needed; if they exceed the limit, ask for approval. The human resource department can further assist by codifying these practices, relating them to specific job-related behaviors that constitute cause for dismissal or discipline, and informing staff about standards of conduct.

Some forms of misconduct, such as chronic lateness, abuse of sick leave or vacation time, and unapproved absences may be symptoms of other problems. The manager may need to consult with the human resource department about seeking the advice of the Employee Assistance Program (EAP) coordinator to help diagnose the situation and provide a reasonable approach to resolving the problem. (See discussion of EAP below.) In some cases, solutions and alternatives such as having the employee work a flextime schedule to resolve child-care or class-scheduling problems, or having the employee attend a time management seminar to better handle the requirements of multiple goals (e.g., career, family, education) may be viable. The employee is then responsible for making the appropriate changes in behavior to comply with organizational policy or the requirements of an agreement reached with the manager. The human resource department can assist the manager and employee by letting them know what previous solutions have been within the range of acceptable past practices of the organization.

If chronic problems persist, the manager may work with the human resource department to request medical verification of illnesses or, perhaps, to arrange a medical examination of the employee to determine fitness for duty. It may also be necessary for the human resource department to determine if unauthorized leave time or absences should be deducted from the employee's pay. These actions are usually taken in situations where excessive use or abuse has occurred.

JOB-RELATED PROBLEMS

The workplace is a positive environment for most workers. It is where competence can be demonstrated and hard work appreciated. It can be the place where workers grow and strengthen their personal and professional identities. However, some employees experience the workplace quite differently. They may feel that their individuality is stifled; they are underappreciated; they are treated like an interchangeable part rather than a person; they are forced to blindly follow an authority hierarchy that was not of their choosing; and their professional judgment has little weight against petty office politics. For some workers, this alternative experience manifests itself as stress, anger, boredom, burnout, or reduced motivation. When these symptoms affect work performance, the manager must deal with the underlying cause, which often lies within the organizational setting itself. The reasons for these responses are varied. They may involve disappointment about promotional opportunities, conflict with coworkers, loss of trust or confidence in the supervisor or administration, lack of challenge in the job, or reactions to demands for continuously high levels of output and long work hours. These are issues that are often beyond the realm of most front-line managers to resolve. Because these problems often affect the productivity and morale of groups of employees, department managers and the human resource department need to work together using a systems approach.

Governmental organizations that are prone to crisis management typically do not devote sufficient time to worker needs. Under these circumstances, dysfunctional relationships between managers and staff can easily develop and lead to disruptive behavior as subtle as taking "mental health" days or as overt as inciting others to protest working conditions by staging a "sickout." It would be easy to view these disruptions in the workplace as individual acts of disobedience or sabotage caused by disgruntled workers, who deserve to be disciplined. However, the end result of job-related problems is often a toxic work environment that cannot be repaired by dealing with individuals. The human resource department can help managers gain a larger perspective of what is happening in the work environment by conducting organizational climate surveys, sharing information gathered from exit interviews, and hiring organizational development (OD) experts to assess the organizational culture to understand why it is no longer conducive to productivity, individual growth, and respect for one another. The human resource department often has the tools to identify these systems issues and by being removed from daily operations, they can also see patterns of behavior that department managers are unaware of because they are too close to the situation.

ORGANIZATIONAL ASSISTANCE PROGRAMS

Although EAPs exist for workers, organizational assistance programs do not currently exist formally for organizations. However, many organizations use a variety of approaches to help resolve internal problems. Some have instituted internal team-building programs. Employing professionals who function like internal consultants, these programs aim to provide organizational development and training that can help resolve problems and nurture viable work groups. Others employ outside consultants to assist when specific problems have been identified. Employee advisory boards and ombudspersons are used in some institutions to provide opportunities for employees to identify problems and have them resolved with executive-level managers. Practices such as Total Quality Management (TQM) and self-directed work teams (SDWTs) have contributed to better problem-solving approaches in many public agencies.

Organizations that have employees in positions such as police officers, social workers, psychotherapists, teachers, and nurses, may develop specific programs to address organizational dysfunction, burnout, or corruption. Universities, school districts, and some businesses have instituted sabbaticals to promote professional development and renewal. Still others have implemented new management approaches such as "empowerment" or "power sharing" that actively involve employees in all aspects of work-related decision making. The Navy, for example, has spent considerable time training its officers in Total Quality Leadership, a variant of Total Quality Management.

Many organizations have done little to respond to institutionally based problems. This situation can lead to a loss of valuable employees and the persistence of organizational dysfunction. At a minimum, human resource departments can conduct exit interviews with employees who are leaving the organization to determine whether specific patterns exist within departments or throughout the agency. This information can serve as a starting point for executive-level discussion, decision making, and problem solving.

PERSONAL PROBLEMS

Our sense of well-being involves an intricate linkage between our personal lives and our professional lives. It is no surprise that when we have problems at work, we take them home, and when we have personal problems, we take them to the office. Family problems, as well as emotional or physical illnesses, tend to intensify existing work-related stress to the point of jeopardizing job performance. Some employees may become depressed or attempt to handle personal problems through excessive use of alcohol, prescription medication, or illegal drugs, but to no avail. As a result, many public sector organizations through their human resource departments have established EAPs to assist managers in resolving personal problems that have an impact on employee performance and job-related behavior.

Since department managers are not expected to assume the role of a trained therapist, the EAP coordinator helps them identify specific behaviors displayed by employees with problems. The EAP coordinator may also provide advice on how to approach discussions and agreements with employees. In most organizations, sending employees to an EAP does not excuse them from any pending disciplinary action. Hence, any agreement between managers and employees should be in writing so that the connection between resolving personal problems and improving performance is clear.

Prior to discussing the suspected personal problems of an employee, the manager needs to clearly identify how the employee's behavior is affecting the worker's job or the work of others in the unit. With the assistance of the human resource department and the EAP coordinator, the manager can identify the problem and explore alternative courses of action.

With regard to personal problems such as depression and drug or alcohol abuse, the supervisor may refer the employee to the EAP or the employee may seek the assistance of an EAP coordinator independently. The EAP coordinator acts as a confidential service broker by referring employees to various services, programs, or treatment centers to receive assistance in resolving the problem. Organizations that participate in these programs generally allow employees to use their mental health or medical plans, where appropriate, and leave time to receive treatment. In organizations where there is a zero tolerance of substance abuse, an employee may only get one chance at a rehabilitation program. Before returning, employees sign a contract indicating the terms and conditions for reinstatement or continued employment.

Participation in an EAP is both confidential and voluntary. The manager does not need to know what was discussed between therapist and worker. All the manager needs to know is that the worker's performance is improving. In the end, the employee is ultimately responsible for meeting the job requirements and actively working to resolve the problems that led to unsatisfactory productivity or inappropriate job behaviors. An employee should be encouraged, but cannot be forced, to attend an EAP because therapists do not believe that change will be genuine or forthcoming if coerced. If the employee refuses the recommendation to participate in an EAP, that is not grounds for further disciplinary action. The bottom line is that if performance improvements are not made, whether an EAP is attended or not, managers must deal with the substandard performance and the employee must live with the consequences.

ETHICAL CONDUCT

Misconduct involving theft, abuse of resources or property, falsification of records, and criminal activity, generally involve more immediate and severe action than found in the normal discipline process. Although due process procedures must be observed, managers can generally move to suspend or discharge an employee without lengthy counseling processes and conferences—especially if the employee has signed a document acknowledging receipt and knowledge of a zero tolerance policy toward specific offenses.

Even in these situations, the manager must still exercise caution and consider the total circumstances surrounding the problem. For example, in cases of theft, had the employee really stolen the article or was he or she under the impression that it was being borrowed? Did someone give the employee permission to take the item? Had the employer consistently reminded the employee about the rules regarding such theft or the appearance of impropriety? Were employees in similar circumstances not punished? With regard to altercations between two employees, had one employee been provoked? Consultation with personnel specialists can be very helpful in these instances. Rather than view the personnel department as interfering with discipline or prolonging the disciplinary process, managers should welcome any help that ensures that sufficient documentation is gathered, due process is afforded, and disciplinary procedures are being followed. Failure to do so may result in the proposed discipline being overturned or increased vulnerability to litigation.

In most cases, the organization may choose to take disciplinary action separate and apart from any criminal court prosecution. Except in the case of law enforcement officers, administrative actions may not need to be reexamined if the alleged perpetrator is later found innocent in a court of law. In many human resource systems, the appearance of impropriety may be sufficient grounds for disciplinary action, especially if it adversely affects the organization's reputation or ability to do business.

DISCIPLINE PROCEDURES:
PROGRESSIVE DISCIPLINE VS. POSITIVE DISCIPLINE

PROGRESSIVE DISCIPLINE

In many organizations the traditional progressive discipline approach is used to address persistent employee performance problems.[3] When progressive discipline was developed in the 1930s, it was intended to provide a structured process of coaching, advising, and goal setting aimed at changing nonproductive or impeding employee behavior. The process includes the following steps:

1. *Oral warning*—a verbal warning from the supervisor that improvement in performance or behavior is needed;

2. *Written reprimand*—a written notice from the supervisor that further action will be taken if the employee's performance or behavior does not improve;

3. *Suspension*—temporary removal of the employee from the job (generally without pay)—since this action is considered quite serious, the employee should be provided due process rights;

4. *Demotion*—downgrading the employee's classification and pay; and

5. *Discharge/Termination from Employment*—the employee is permanently dismissed from the organization.

When the progressive discipline process moves to the final step, a manager must face the difficult decision to terminate an employee who has performance or behavior problems. Often managers and supervisors want to move hastily to dismiss such employees in order to replace them with employees who can function as members of the unit. In the public sector, however, this can be a long-term process for permanent or tenured employees since they are generally granted due process rights through the courts, union contracts, or organizational policies. In government organizations, public sector employees have "property rights" with regard to their permanent position and must be given a due process hearing before any disciplinary action is taken.

If the employee is able to overturn the termination in court or arbitration, he or she may be reinstated and receive back pay for lost wages. Therefore, it is incumbent upon the department manager to use appropriate approaches and mechanisms to help resolve employee problems and to work closely with the human resource department so that each step of the process is implemented correctly and in full compliance with laws, regulations, and policies.

Termination of an employee must be done only for "just cause" or "reasonable cause." Just cause is determined by the manager, in consultation with the human resource department and legal office, when the employee has substantially violated one or more of the organization's rules, such as falsifying one's application form, commission of a criminal offense involving moral turpitude, addiction to the use of narcotics or other drugs, using alcohol or drugs while on duty, dishonesty, soliciting or taking for personal use a fee, gift, or other item of value in the course of one's work, excessive absenteeism, misuse of agency property, incompetence in the performance of duty, neglect of duty, and so forth.

POSITIVE DISCIPLINE

Managers in new era organizations are beginning to perceive a conflict between progressive discipline and the new forms of management that involve employee ownership of and commitment to the vision, mission, and values of the organization as well as a move toward flatter organizational structures, employee empowerment, and work teams. Grote argues that coaching and counseling is really not viable in the progressive discipline process because the manager or supervisor inevitably becomes an adversary resulting in hostility and resentment of the employee.[4]

Positive discipline or discipline without punishment is an approach to performance improvement that attempts to recast the process to fit today's organizations. The intent of this process is to have enlightened employees take responsibility for their behavior and performance. Positive discipline begins with informal discussion with the employee and coaching by the supervisor. The formal steps in this process have been reduced to three.

1. *Reminder I*—The supervisor discusses the problem, reminds the employee of his or her responsibility to meet the organization's standards, and gains the employee's agreement to return to fully acceptable performance.

2. *Reminder II*—The supervisor talks to the employee again and gains his or her agreement to solve the problem, then formally documents the discussion in a written memo to the employee.

3. *Decision-Making Leave*—The employee is suspended for one day with pay and asked to return with a decision to perform in every aspect of the job or to resign and seek more satisfying employment elsewhere. The employee is advised that if further problems arise, he or she will be terminated.[5]

Government agencies such as Mecklenburg County, the City of Carrollton, Texas, and the State of Georgia have instituted positive discipline or discipline without punishment programs. The Texas Department of Mental Health and Mental Retardation reported that turnover at their agency dropped from 48.5 percent to 18.5 percent in the first two years after implementation of the new procedure.[6] Agencies that have adopted this procedure report that it eliminates the punitive loss of pay, shifts the responsibility from the supervisor to the employee, reduces hostility and risk of workplace violence, and provides a stronger case to a judge or arbitrator that the organization's actions are fair and just to its employees.[7]

GRIEVANCE MANAGEMENT

Despite the best efforts of department and human resource managers to re-solve a performance problem productively and amicably, employees may ex-ercise their right to file a grievance. Generally, employees file a grievance if they believe the discipline or dismissal was unjust or as a last resort to over-turning the manager's decision. Employees may exercise their right to grieve even when managers have made every attempt to implement the performance improvement process properly and have just cause to take a final action. In these cases, the decision by employees to file a formal grievance creates frus-tration and results in a very time-consuming process for department and hu-man resource managers. However, the right to grieve the actions of managers exists to protect employees from improper or unfair actions that may result in job loss or other punitive actions.

The best protection for managers is to assure that the performance improvement process is administered properly and with the best interest of the employee and organization in mind. To a large extent, grievances can be avoided or at least overturned in court by employing sound management practices. Department managers should

1. be thoroughly familiar with performance improvement and grievance policies and know the rights of employees in this procedure;
2. work closely with the human resource department from the beginning of the performance improvement process;
3. be fair, equitable, and consistent in dealings with employees;
4. take a problem-solving attitude toward employee problems, think win-win rather than win-lose, approach each situation with an open mind; and
5. use a people-oriented management style that engenders trust and demonstrates mutual respect.

GRIEVANCE MANAGEMENT IN COLLECTIVE BARGAINING ENVIRONMENTS

Many states and the federal government have laws that grant public sector employees the right to bargain collectively for wages, hours, and other terms and conditions of employment. This includes a negotiated grievance pro-cedure as a part of the contract. With collective bargaining agreements being commonplace in public sector organizations, the department manager must assume a very specific role as an agent of management rather than as the champion of one's workers. While this does not mean that managers should abandon the interests of employees, it is the case that the union becomes the official agent for the worker and department heads are the organization's representatives. This shift in perspective is important because the singular actions of one manager can be seen as either upholding or violating the terms of a negotiated agreement. Therefore, the first and most significant responsibility for the department manager in this arena is to become familiar with the contract.

Most organizations provide workshops for managers to review the language and intent of the agreement as well as to discuss new provisions and changes. However, it is the manager's responsibility to abide by the contract as it is written and not deviate from its terms and provisions. This requires consistency in implementation within the department and throughout the organization. Managers are often inconsistent because they (a) want to play the "nice" manager role, (b) attempt to exercise discretionary authority, or (c) misinterpret the meaning of the contract language. Playing the nice manager or attempting to exercise discretionary authority creates problems for the organization, distrust of managers among employees, and leads to grievances.

Living with a collective bargaining contract produces a certain level of clarity concerning organizational regulations while simultaneously reducing managerial flexibility. Many provisions pertaining to working conditions and other terms are specifically stated so that managers and employees know what is required. Exceptions to these provisions, however, cannot be made by the manager even when there appear to be compelling reasons to do so. If exceptions are made, the union has established cause to file a grievance.

Often contract language is ambiguous despite both parties' best efforts to provide clarity. In some cases, the language is intentionally left vague to avoid stalling the negotiations or is ambiguous due to poor drafting.[8] When the manager encounters this situation, the human resource or employee relations department should be contacted immediately for assistance. The manager should not guess or attempt to provide a personal interpretation. The organization's employee relations experts can explain the intent of the language and indicate how the provision should be interpreted since they were present during the actual negotiations.

Under a collective bargaining contract, a laborer may file a grievance when he or she "believes that management has violated the terms of a labor contract."[9] Grievances should be taken seriously and not dismissed as frivolous gripes because a formal grievance, by definition, must be founded in a violation of the labor-management agreement, a past employment practice, or federal, state, or local law. Grievances may also be an indicator of poor management practices, such as autocratic leadership, favoritism, unsafe working conditions, or discrimination. Grievance procedures provide a mechanism for the employee or union to register a formal complaint and receive a fair hearing.[10] The types of grievances managers most often encounter are those pertaining to disciplinary actions including performance improvement and dismissal from the position, job assignments, promotions, absenteeism, health and safety issues, vacation assignments, discrimination, overtime, layoffs, and reduction in force.[11]

Handling grievances in the public sector is particularly complex due to the multiple avenues for settling disputes available to public employees. Typically, negotiated grievance procedures are used. However, some organizations (e.g., the federal government) provide their employees with an option to choose either a civil service appeal procedure or the negotiated procedure. Employees who file grievances pertaining to allegations of discrimination also have the option to choose an external appeal procedure through agencies such as the Equal Employment Opportunity Commission as well as state and local compliance agencies.

Negotiated grievance procedures usually include a minimum of three levels or steps—the informal complaint to the immediate supervisor; a formal, written appeal to the department head or equivalent; and final, binding arbitration by a neutral third party who is jointly appointed by labor and management. The goal of the grievance process is to have the complaint resolved at the earliest stage. This generally keeps problems from escalating and is the least expensive process for both parties. Thus, it is not uncommon to find that a grievance must be filed within a specified time of the alleged grievable event. If not filed within the specified time, the ability to grieve is forfeited. If grieved, the department supervisor may have only a few working days to respond to the grievant. If the supervisor does not respond in a timely fashion, the grievant may seek remedy or have the basis for a further grievance. Should the supervisor respond within the specified time frame and the grievant not be satisfied with the response, the grievant may have only a short time frame (perhaps only three to five working days) to appeal the response to the next level. The next level of the grievance process then starts a new round of tight time frames.

Effective communication is a major key to early resolution of complaints at the informal stage. In this case, effective communication specifically involves objectivity, effective listening, fact-finding, and time lines. Objectivity in a grievance situation requires the supervisor to remain focused on the problem or issue with the intent of seeking a resolution, as opposed to viewing the situation as a personal affront or criticism. Effective listening involves a concerted effort by the supervisor to determine the employee's perception of the problem. Once the supervisor understands the problem, he or she should collect pertinent facts concerning the situation beginning with an understanding and interpretation of the applicable contract language. Finally, the supervisor should communicate the decision concerning the complaint to the employee as expeditiously as possible.

PEER REVIEW GRIEVANCE PROCEDURES

Employees in nonunion environments that use positive discipline programs can elect to use a peer review grievance process when they cannot resolve a problem with their supervisor. Peer review is a formal grievance process for resolving common disputes in the organization, which ends in final and binding resolution of the problem. The panel in most agencies includes three peers and two managers who are trained volunteers.

The process typically consists of several steps:

- employee presentation of his or her case including recommendations for resolution of the problem;
- collection of information by the panel by asking questions, interviewing witnesses, researching precedents, and reviewing policy;
- agreement on final decision by majority vote; and
- transmittal of decision and explanation in writing to the employee.[12]

According to management consultant Dick Grote, public sector agencies that use a peer review system indicate that there are several advantages to this approach in nonunion environments.[13] Managers are more likely to think through their actions and avoid indefensible decisions. A panel that includes the employees' peers as the majority members hears employees' complaints. The panel consists of insiders who know the organization. The organization makes a concerted effort to balance employee and management rights and responsibilities. Finally, the problem is resolved permanently; and the system prevents most grievances from ever going to court.

WORKSHOP 5

Managing Performance Improvement

PRE-SERVICE OR IN-SERVICE STUDENTS

Progressive Discipline

Instructions:

Prior to the workshop, students should go online to search various city, county, or state websites, search the government document library holdings, or visit local human resource departments to gather lists of causes for dismissal, demotion, and suspension as well as documents listing specified consequences for infractions. In addition, gather copies of the agencies' grievance procedures. Form small groups of approximately five members to conduct the workshop.

Part I—Cause

In small groups, compare and contrast the lists of causes. Which causes are most frequently mentioned? Which causes appear to be most serious? Translate the top five causes into observable behavior that would be understood by both workers and department managers.

Part 2—Consequences

In small groups, compare and contrast the list of consequences for each type of infraction. What are the typical consequences for a first-time offense, second offense, and third offense for a worker who has excessive tardiness? What are the typical consequences for misconduct that is of a serious nature? Make a list of mitigating circumstances that might excuse or reduce a consequence for low productivity.

Part 3—Handling Grievances

Grievance administration is a complex topic that involves both matters of procedure and the art of resolving differences. The goal of this exercise is for students to better understand the grievance process and to develop alternative strategies for handling grievances.

Format:

Students may work independently or in teams.

Research:

Conduct Internet or library research on grievance procedures and grievance administration. Interview or e-mail one of the following:

- civil service commission administrator;
- human resource specialist responsible for grievance administration;
- manager who has handled a grievance;
- union representative who handles grievances; or
- employee who has filed a grievance.

Classroom Discussion:

Discuss the following issues:

- What types of grievances are filed?
- What is the most frequently cited grievance?
- What are the steps in the grievance process?
- What are the rules regarding responsiveness and timeliness?
- Why are grievances denied or sustained?
- How should grievances be handled? What strategies and tactics are recommended?
- How can grievances be prevented?
- What improvements or changes are needed to improve the efficacy of grievance administration?

Positive Discipline or Discipline without Punishment

Divide into groups of four to five. Search the Internet to identify government agencies that practice the positive discipline or discipline without punishment method of performance improvement (e.g., Mecklenburg County, the City of Carrollton, Texas, and the State of Georgia) and use peer review grievance procedures.

- Compare the policies and procedures among different agencies. What are the differences and commonalties?
- Discover the strengths and weaknesses of the program from information on the agency's website and/or e-mail correspondence with the human resource manager.
- Does the group think that most government agencies should adopt the positive discipline and peer review procedures? Why or why not?
- Each group should share its findings with the class.

Employee Assistance Programs (EAPs)

EAPs play an important role in reducing the impact of personal and work-related stress on job performance. There are a variety of programs and approaches. Students can learn from both public and private sector practices.

Format:

Students may work individually or in groups. Present an example of an exemplary EAP from an agency or company's website or by contacting the organizations directly.

- Describe the features of the program.
- What problems/issues does the program address?
- Who is eligible to participate in the program?
- How does one elect to participate?
- What makes each program unique or different from other EAP programs?
- What are the costs and benefits for implementing the program?
- What are the similarities and differences between public and private programs?
- Which agencies or companies appear to have the best programs? What distinguishes their programs?
- Which agencies or companies appear to have programs that need improvement? What do they need to do to strengthen their programs?
- What are some of the benefits and pitfalls of having EAPs in public organizations?

- Will employees in all job categories benefit from the program or are there some categories of employees that are likely to be more resistant to using the program than others?

NOTES

1. Paul Hersey, Kenneth H. Blanchard, and Dewey E. Johnson. *Management of Organizational Behavior: Utilizing Human Resources* (Upper Saddle River, NJ: Prentice Hall, 1996), 188.

2. Ibid., 67.

3. Ibid., 278–296.

4. Dick Grote, *Public Sector Organizations: Today's Innovative Leaders in Performance Management,* in IPMA [database online] (Alexandria, VA: IPMA, December 1999 [cited 8 March 2000]), member-restricted access at http://www.ipma-hr.org.

5. Ibid.

6. Ibid.

7. Ibid.

8. E. Allan Farnsworth, *Contracts,* 3d ed. (New York: Aspen, 1999), 457.

9. Pynes, *Human Resources Management,* 244.

10. Ban and Riccucci, *Public Personnel Management: Current Concerns, Future Challenges,* 162–163.

11. Richard C. Kearney, *Labor Relations in the Public Sector,* 2d ed. (New York: M. Dekker, 1992), 373.

12. Ibid.

13. Ibid.

6

EMPLOYEE SAFETY AND HEALTH

Department managers and human resource specialists share the responsibility for safety policies and health programs. Because the human resource department traditionally has been delegated the responsibility for keeping records of work-related injuries, administering health and disability programs, and training employees, it is easy to assume that the human resource department alone should be responsible for safety and health programs in government organizations. Indeed, the human resource department commonly provides safety instruction during basic orientation training, develops safety awareness and disaster preparedness programs, and refers troubled employees to the appropriate employee assistance program because it can access the needed expertise and coordinate across divisions and units.

However, department managers play a key role in the success of these safety and health programs. Managers may be surprised to learn that most work-related injuries are not caused by employees who are unaware of safety rules or careless in the application of proper methods of operation, but are the result of workers performing unsafe acts in direct violation of organization policies. If managers assume that safety education is the responsibility of human resource trainers, the opportunity to transfer knowledge from training to the work site and to reinforce safe work practices is in jeopardy. Department managers set the tone for safety and health in the workplace by making them clear and unquestioned priorities, by setting, championing, and enforcing the highest safety and health standards, and by holding themselves and subordinates accountable for accident and injury prevention.

Lack of attention to safety and health issues in the workplace is a luxury that few organizations can afford. When workers are injured, productivity suffers. The injured worker will need time away from work to seek treatment, to obtain needed rehabilitation, and to recover. Managers will spend countless hours investigating the circumstances that led to the injury, writing reports, and consulting with risk managers and lawyers, if need be. Morale and general productivity in the organization may also be affected as other workers speculate about what happened, who will be the next "victim," and whether managers could and should have prevented the injury. When other workers have to fill in for absent workers, stress may accumulate and further disrupt efficiency and effectiveness. If the stressed-out workers use their health-care benefits, are absent from work due to stress-related illness, or are granted a stress disability leave, the employer's share of health-care premiums will undoubtedly increase in subsequent contract years. If the injured worker files a worker's compensation claim, operational costs are increased (especially if the organization is self-insured) and the organization may become the subject of state and federal health and safety regulators, a union grievance, or a lawsuit. If state and federal investigators find against the organization, substantial fines could be levied, and an expensive redesign of the workplace could be required. In a worst-case scenario, conviction on charges of criminal negligence could result in prison sentences for those held responsible.

As the workforce continues to age, managers may find that some older workers have more costly health-related problems that accompany the aging process. Because the Age Discrimination in Employment Act of 1967 prohibits discriminating against older workers and the Americans with Disabilities Act of 1990 prohibits discriminating against persons with self-defined disabilities, it is not appropriate or legal to replace them. Managers cannot, of course, force them to retire, since that would be a violation of the provisions of the Age Discrimination in Employment Act of 1967.

A safe and healthy workplace is not the sole responsibility of human resources. The time and energy required for department managers to work in conjunction with human resources to implement sound safety and health policies will be returned manyfold in increased job satisfaction, higher productivity, and lower fiscal and emotional costs. This chapter is designed to help department managers develop a sound strategy for establishing and maintaining a safe and healthy workplace.

SAFETY HAZARDS VS. HEALTH HAZARDS

Although often appearing together, safety and health hazards have very distinct connotations to those involved with risk management. Safety hazards refer to injuries that impair the employee's physical well-being. Thus, managers need to pay attention to hazards that may cause potential injuries such as telephone cords that might be tripped over, overloaded extension cords that might cause an electric shock or start a fire, and coffeepots, fax machines, and copiers that may cause burns. Attention should also be paid to hazards that may potentially cause back, arm, and leg injuries due to overexertion while moving and picking up objects, fingers caught in file drawers and machinery, and head injuries from falling objects, such as books falling off shelves. Occupational injuries may also include cuts, fractures, sprains, dismemberment, insect bites, and animal bites.

Occupational diseases are usually the result of long-term exposure to health hazards, such as the absorption of chemicals through the skin, repeated exposure to radiation, inhaling cancer-causing asbestos particles from water pipe insulation and ceiling tiles, hearing loss from noisy working conditions, and so on. Health hazards resulting in occupational disease are often difficult to discern and are usually detected only after extensive statistical research.

Lawsuits brought by nuclear reactor inspectors and workers who claimed that they developed unusual forms of leukemia and cancer because of long-time exposure to "nuclear fleas" rely heavily upon showing a high statistical improbability, when compared to the general population, that they contracted cancer by any other means. Nuclear fleas are radioactive particles so small that they are undetectable by standard detection methods. The afflicted workers assert that standard decontamination methods do not protect them against these nuclear fleas.

With more employees working on computer keyboards today, particular attention must be paid to repetitive motion injuries—injuries that result from repeating the same movements without a break. Carpal tunnel syndrome, which causes pain and numbness in the hand as well as loss of grip strength due to swollen tendons pressing on vital nerves in the wrist, was not a problem in the past because typing involved other motions besides keystrokes—moving the typewriter carriage back and forth, inserting and removing paper, erasing mistakes, and so forth.

Unfortunately, the tendency for some managers is to dismiss worker concerns about possible safety and health hazards in the workplace. In regard to safety, department managers may blame the worker for not using common sense, not using prudent caution, or not following established safety rules. Yet while managers may hold the worker accountable through a negative performance evaluation, the organization still has a work-related injury that it must deal with. Even though an office worker who burns a hand trying to fix a paper jam inside a photocopier should have known better, a worker's compensation injury report still must be filled out, the incident investigated, and appropriate treatment sought at the organization's expense.

Dealing with worker concerns about health hazards are even more difficult due to the lack of a clear connection between cause and effect, the possibility that the resultant illness or injury may have non-job-related origins, and the fear that implying any culpability now may lead to future legal litigation. For example, as personal computers have become commonplace in government offices as important productivity tools, so have complaints about their effects on workers. Are worker complaints about eyestrain, headaches, and the loss of visual acuity the result of being bombarded by an electron-emitting video display terminal (VDT) that is four feet closer than the normal distance from a television screen? Or could the aging process, an incorrect eye prescription, or some other condition be a factor? Should women in childbearing years, much less pregnant women, expose themselves to the low frequency electromagnetic fields of the VDT and computer itself? Lacking research data one way or the other, if managers issue a cautionary warning or limit the number of hours of exposure to VDTs, even with the best of intentions, are managers needlessly admitting to possible future liability?

Health and safety involve complexities that require the best thinking of both human resource administrators and department managers in order to deal with real work hazards, prevent future accidents and injuries, and investigate potential occupational diseases. A number of laws have been passed that structure the way in which managers can and must govern safety and health in the workplace.

STATE AND FEDERAL LAW

The industrial revolution radically altered American social and economic life, including how managers deal with health and safety issues in the workplace. The industrial revolution meant that prosperity beyond the subsistence existence of an agrarian society was now literally in the hands of both business owners and workers who could use tools and machinery more efficiently than in past eras—but not without a cost. Workplace injuries were commonplace in industrial America. Machines were designed to maximize efficiency, not safety. In a market economy, workers were replaceable. Those injured were not compensated and families of those killed were not financially remunerated.

It was only after several well-publicized industrial disasters, such as the fire that needlessly killed a number of female garment workers unable to use a locked fire escape, that states began to pass worker safety and worker's compensation laws. Workers could now be compensated for lost income while injured, have medical and rehabilitative services paid for, receive lump sum payments for permanent disability, and obtain death benefits for survivors. Workers who received compensation, however, gave up their right to sue the employer and were limited in what they could receive by state law.

At the federal level, Congress struggled for more than a century to develop a comprehensive workplace safety bill that balanced employee and employer rights and obligations. Finally in 1970, the Occupational Safety and Health Act was passed. This legislation centralized the regulation of workplace safety and expanded the number of organizations covered by these regulations. Recognizing that there were differences between states, this act allows states to administer their own occupational safety and health programs so long as these programs are federally approved and include federal safety standards. About half the states have opted for their own programs and some have more stringent requirements than the federal standards. One advantage of state safety and health programs is that they allow employers to seek voluntary advice about safety and health requirements. Under the federal system, such an inquiry might lead to an unwanted full investigation.

The Occupational Safety and Health Act created three agencies to ensure that the workplace was free from recognized hazards that could cause injury or illness to workers. The National Institute for Occupational Safety and Health (NIOSH) is located in the Department of Health and Human Services. Its job is to conduct and coordinate research on workplace safety and health. For example, NIOSH might conduct studies on the effects of different workplace noise levels on hearing loss, the levels of acceptable particulate matter that workers can breathe or touch without causing illness, the impact of lighting on visual acuity, and so on, in order to make recommendations about safety and health standards. These findings can provide managers with valuable information that can be used to build a safer and healthier workplace.

The Occupational Safety and Health Review Commission (OSHRC) is administered by the Department of Labor. Organizations can appeal safety and health citations to OSHRC. OSHRC attempts to take an impartial judicial role in administering health and safety regulations. Dissatisfied appellants may file suit in the federal court system.

Of the three agencies responsible for worker safety and health, the most visible is the Occupational Safety and Health Administration (OSHA) located in the Department of Labor. OSHA is responsible for creating health and safety standards and enforcing these regulations at the national level. While a risk-free work environment was the original policy standard for OSHA, Supreme Court decisions over the years have established that the standard should be primarily safety, not zero risk.

On-site OSHA inspections are most likely when reports have been received that workers are in imminent danger, that fatalities may be linked to working conditions, and that worker complaints about unsafe or unhealthy work conditions have been validated. OSHA may also target certain industries that have a high rate of accidents or sites where there have been chronic problems with worker safety and health.

Often in conjunction with managers and union representatives, OSHA inspectors visit a work site looking for unsafe and unhealthy working conditions. If an OSHA standard has been violated, a citation can be issued and the organization ordered to fix the problem by a certain date. If the problem continues, OSHA can fine the organization. Consequently, department managers must make sure that workers and supervisors fully comply with safety requirements.

Under OSHA regulations, there are several types of violations. *Willful violations* of OSHA regulations, especially those that lead to an employee's death, may result in criminal prosecution, a fine not to exceed $10,000, and/or a prison term up to six months. A willful violation suggests that the perpetrator deliberately, intentionally, and consciously engaged in an act that showed indifference toward worker safety or carelessly disregarded OSHA requirements. *Repeat violations* of OSHA standards may lead to fines of $10,000 per offense. *Nonserious violations* are violations of OSHA requirements that would probably not lead to serious physical harm or death. Fines cannot be imposed unless there is a history of ten or more such violations. The maximum penalty is $10,000. *De minimus violations* are the least serious violations. A notice, rather than a citation, is issued, and there are no penalties attached.

Organizations may be exempt from random OSHA inspections if there is a management-worker safety committee that responds to worker complaints, holds regular monthly safety self-inspections, and gathers and analyzes statistical data. An effective management-worker safety committee is empowered to investigate complaints, cite violators, require mandatory safety training and/or competency for transgressors and those who are accident-prone, and develop a comprehensive safety and health plan for the organization.

A GENERAL STRATEGY

Besides establishing a management-worker safety committee, managers can take a number of other strategies to establish and maintain a safe and healthy work environment. As indicated earlier in this chapter, the first step in any serious strategy to eliminate accidents and injuries from the workplace is for managers to make safety and health issues a top priority. When managers take health and safety issues seriously, so will others in the organization. Managers can motivate staff to abide by safety rules by establishing awards and incentives for units that demonstrate a low rate of injury and illness. It is critically important, however, that managers enforce health and safety policies by making the safety and health of workers a measurable performance objective in the performance review of its staff.

The second step is for executive managers to clearly delegate responsibility and appropriate authority to human resource and department managers to implement and enforce safety policies and procedures. In most instances, the human resource department is responsible for gathering data on occupational injuries and designing safety and health policies and programs, while department managers are responsible for implementing safety procedures in the workplace. For this division of labor to work, human resource and department managers must cooperate and coordinate their efforts. Department managers are then not afraid to report accidents and request safety information from the human resource department, and, in turn, the human resource manager is not reluctant to make recommendations about improving safety practices to department managers.

A third step is to have a sound safety training program that instructs workers about safety procedures. New workers are particularly prone to accidents and injuries on the job because they lack training and experience to identify work hazards. While human resource trainers are usually responsible for conducting the training, supervisors must also be trained to identify safe work methods so that unsafe performance can be identified and stopped. Supervisors also play an important role in demonstrating to workers that safety procedures learned in training must be used at the actual work site. Vigilance is even more critical when there has not been an accident within recent memory. Without ongoing feedback and motivation from managers, it is not uncommon for workers to ignore seemingly cumbersome safety procedures because there appear to be no negative consequences for not following the rules.

Fourth, since OSHA requires employers to keep records of all occupational injuries and illnesses that result in death, loss of consciousness, transfer of duties, medical treatment beyond emergency first aid, and lost work time, managers should regularly review those records with the human resource department to determine if there has been a change in the rate of reported incidents. An increase suggests that additional safety and health precautions need to be taken; a decrease may suggest that successful programs have been implemented and those responsible need to be recognized for their achievements. Regardless of the incidence rate, any pattern of injuries or illnesses within certain organizational units may suggest the necessity for an internal investigation, report, and subsequent plan of action.

Finally, managers can prevent accidents, injuries, and occupational disease in the workplace by involving workers in identifying safety and health issues. At a minimum, informing workers is not only a good management strategy but required by OSHA regulations. In 1986, OSHA promulgated new hazard communication rules—better known as "right-to-know" regulations. Employers are required to provide workers with information about the hazardous substances that they may encounter on the job as they go about their normal duties. Managers are required to post statements on work site bulletin boards that employees have the right to request information about toxic substances in the work area. The notice must also state that there can be no reprisals for employees exercising their right to know. Managers are required to maintain material safety data sheets (MSDS) that list the types and locations of hazardous materials. Toxic substances stored in containers must be labeled and workers should be trained on the safe handling of the materials, including what to do when unduly exposed to the substances and what to do in cases of emergency. In some states that have their own federally approved OSHA requirements, fire marshals, public health officials, doctors, and area residents may also have a right to know about hazardous materials in the workplace.

SUBSTANCE ABUSE

Substance abuse is a pernicious problem plaguing our society. It is therefore no surprise that substance abuse and all of its associated problems also exist in the workplace. It has been suggested that substance abuse, whether excessive alcohol consumption, the use of illegal drugs, or the abuse of prescription drugs, has an adverse impact on the workplace because substance abusers are prone to more accidents and more frequent absences. They are unable to perform at a consistently productive level, and they may be engaged in some aspect of white-collar crime to support their habit.

In 1988, Congress passed the Drug Free Workplace Act. Federal contractors and grantees that receive more than $25,000 in federal grants or contracts must, as a condition for receiving the funds, declare that they are, and will remain, a drug-free workplace. As a result of this act, managers in most governmental agencies are required to establish a drug-free workplace policy. The policy must notify employees that they are prohibited from the illegal use, possession, manufacture, and distribution of controlled substances in the workplace. The policy must also warn employees that violators will be dealt with sternly. Because remaining drug-free is a mandatory requirement for employment under this act, employees must notify the employer within five days if they are convicted of a drug-related crime. The human resource department is, in turn, then required to notify the federal contracting agency within ten days of receiving the conviction information.

The act further requires that managers make a good-faith effort to maintain a drug-free work environment. At a minimum, management is required to provide a drug-awareness program to educate workers about the dangers of substance abuse as well as where they can go for help if they are addicted.

Interestingly, the Drug Free Workplace Act does not require mandatory drug testing of current or prospective employees. Although there appears to be legal precedent for it—especially for jobs that involve public safety and transportation—there seems to be little question that mandatory preemployment drug testing is a valid business necessity. In the 1978 case of *New York City Transit Authority v Baezer* (440 U.S. 568), the United States Supreme Court found that the safety and efficiency of public transportation constituted a valid business necessity and justifiable reason for requiring drug testing of bus driver applicants. In 1989, the National Labor Relations Board ruled that the Minneapolis *Star-Tribune* could demand that new job applicants be drug tested even though the matter had not been negotiated with the affected labor union.

Mandatory drug testing of regular employees remains a subject of debate. On the one hand, the Fourth and Fourteenth Amendments to the Constitution protect workers from illegal search and seizure by government. Having to give up a urine or blood sample for drug testing is also problematic because it presumes everyone is guilty until his or her innocence is proven. Given the fact that traces of certain illegal drugs may stay in one's system for up to thirty days, mandatory random drug testing also raises the issue about whether employers have the right to regulate the leisure time activities of employees.

On the other hand, the Fourth and Fourteenth Amendments are not absolute rights. In the 1976 Supreme Court case of *Division 241, Amalgamated Transit Union (AFL-CIO) v Suscy et al.* (429 U.S. 1029), the Court decided that the Chicago Transit Authority not only had the right to require blood and urine tests of employees involved in serious traffic accidents but had a duty to protect the public interest by ensuring that bus and train operators were fit to perform their jobs.

Fitness for duty was the rationale used by the military in the late 1960s and early 1970s to drug test GIs before they returned from Vietnam. In the military system, a commander can order a drug test if there is "reasonable suspicion"—such as an unauthorized absence, arrest for drug-related charges, crimes of violence, or disobedience of direct orders. If the drug test is positive, the finding can be used in administrative actions such as discharge from the service. Furthermore, if there is "probable cause" (specific objective facts or rational inferences based on facts) that drug abuse has occurred, such as the soldier appearing intoxicated, then a positive drug test may be entered into evidence in a court-martial.

Mandatory random drug testing of civilian federal employees first occurred in the Reagan administration. Executive Order 12564 prohibited drug use by federal employees and directed agency heads to establish guidelines for mandatory drug testing of employees in so-called sensitive positions—national security, health specialties, hazardous occupations, and law enforcement. Thus far, the Supreme Court has supported this policy by permitting mandatory random drug testing for those involved in public safety positions.

Executive Order 12564 encouraged, but did not force, federal employees in other categories to submit to voluntary drug testing to prove they were drug-free. The Supreme Court has been less willing to sanction mandatory random drug testing for civilian workers in nonsensitive positions. The previously mentioned military standards of reasonable suspicion and probable cause appear to be the only justifications permissible at this time for requiring drug testing of these categories of government employees. Reasonable suspicion may arise when a supervisor becomes aware of such things as erratic behavior, poor work performance, increased absenteeism, or accidents in the workplace. If evidence shows that an employee had alcohol on the breath, had a nonreactive pupillary response, or was observed to use or distribute controlled substances, then the conditions are met for probable cause.

Besides ensuring adherence to the requirements of the Drug-free Workplace Act, managers can also engage in other strategies to ensure a safe and healthy work environment. First, managers need to be trained to identify the typical symptoms of substance abuse. Second, supervisors need to be able to recognize when an intoxicated worker has crossed over the line between acceptable work performance and impaired capacity. Union representatives are likely to argue that testing positive for drugs is not sufficient proof of on-the-job impairment. If managers have been thinking ahead, they may have already identified and contracted with providers who can test pupillary reaction or eye-hand coordination. Both tests are noninvasive.

Third, if there is a policy for drug testing when an accident occurs (or if there is probable cause), workers must be warned that there will be mandatory testing, especially if refusal to take a drug test is cause for immediate termination.

Fourth, drug counseling and drug rehabilitation should be an integral part of a comprehensive employee assistance program. Rarely does substance abuse affect the employee in isolation. Substance abuse is often connected to family and financial problems, and it can sometimes lead to domestic violence, child abuse, and other forms of antisocial behavior. Alcoholism, in particular, also may involve coworkers. While these matters are not the responsibility of managers, good drug counseling programs may go far to alleviate some of these problems to the benefit of all concerned.

Finally, as with other safety and health programs, managers should involve workers themselves in the creation of a drug-free workplace, since managers are not the only ones who benefit.

COMMUNICABLE DISEASES

Many infectious diseases (tuberculosis, meningitis, and hepatitis A) that were expected to be extinct by the twenty-first century still present health risks in today's workplace. In order to handle this problem, human resource and department managers need to address the concerns of three different parties— the infected employee, the employee's coworkers, and the interest of the employer.[1] The infected employee has certain privacy rights and the disease may qualify as a "disability" under the Americans with Disabilities Act of 1990 (ADA). An employer may request that an employee submit to a medical examination if the medical condition is affecting the employee's ability to do his or her job or if the communicable disease poses a "direct threat" to coworkers.[2]

Employers have the responsibility to provide a safe and healthy workplace for all employees while protecting the interest of the infected worker. Given the complexity of this situation, human resource managers should develop a plan for reducing the risks of communicable diseases in the workplace and make provisions for the infected employee to receive a medical leave or provide other reasonable accommodations under the ADA or Family and Medical Leave Act of 1993 (FMLA).[3]

AIDS/HIV

AIDS is considered a disability under the Americans with Disabilities Act of 1990. It is a life-threatening illness to the employee who is infected though there are treatments and medications that help to prolong life and improve health. Current medical and scientific evidence indicates that AIDS or HIV is not transmitted through casual personal contact under normal working conditions and does not pose a risk to the health and safety of coworkers or public sector clientele.[4] Many human resource departments provide policies or guidelines to managers in order to help them respond appropriately to the needs of employees with AIDS or HIV and answer the concerns of coworkers.[5] One sample policy contains the following provisions:

- Managers should be sensitive to the special needs of employees and assist them by demonstrating personal support, referring them to counseling services and arranging for benefits counseling as necessary.

- Coworkers will be expected to continue working relationships with an employee who has AIDS or HIV infection.

- An employee with AIDS or HIV infection is under no obligation to disclose his or her condition to a manager or any other employee.

- An employee with AIDS or HIV infection is expected to meet the same performance requirements applicable to other employees, with reasonable accommodation if necessary.

- Reasonable accommodation may include, but is not limited to, flexible or part-time work schedules, leave of absence, work restructuring or job reassignment.[6]

Human resource managers need to contact legal counsel when developing policies on AIDS/HIV in the workplace. They should also remain current on the latest medical research on AIDS/HIV to revise policies accordingly and to provide guidance to managers and workers.

SMOKE-FREE WORKPLACES

Most public sector employers have adopted policies that regulate smoking in the workplace due to health warnings and medical evidence about the hazards of smoking and secondhand smoke. "Slightly more than 80 percent of workers are covered by an official workplace smoking policy, according to a study sponsored by the National Cancer Institute."[7] Many federal, state, and local governments have established rules and passed laws or ordinances that prohibit smoking in federal, state, or municipal buildings, and some organizations have adopted policies stating that they hire only nonsmokers unless prohibited by law.[8] Several general guidelines apply to the development of workplace smoking policies although these policies vary among employers—research health literature, surveys, and the policies of other employers; review state law and local ordinances; form an employee task force; develop and implement the policy; and evaluate the policy's effectiveness and success.

STRESS IN THE WORKPLACE

The right amount of stress can be invigorating—heightening the senses and improving productivity. Too little stress and there is little desire to be anything but stagnant. Too much stress, on the other hand, may cause psychological, physiological, and behavioral symptoms that managers and the human resource department must deal with. What the optimal level of stress is for each employee, work group, and organization is difficult to determine. Managers will find that some workers will say the stress level is comfortable and others will complain it is too high or too low.

Stress that is present in the workplace is often considered a result of organizational pressures—excessive productivity goals, convoluted organizational politics, enigmatic communication patterns, idiosyncratic management styles, and oppressive rules and regulations. However, a more comprehensive definition of job stress must include stress that is present in other aspects of an employee's life. Employee performance can be affected by personal crises, such as the prolonged illness of a spouse, death of a child, financial insolvency, substance abuse, or mental illness. There is a dynamic interaction between stress at work and stress at home. Workplace pressures can be brought home and vice versa. A bad day at the office could lead to verbal and physical abuse at home; a bad night at home may lead to conflict in the workplace and mistreatment of subordinates and fellow employees, who then expand the cycle of stress by infecting others at home and at work.

How can department and human resource managers work together to deal with worker stress? The first thing to recognize is that stress does not always make itself readily apparent in the workplace. Workers themselves may not even be aware of its presence. Job stress may easily remain hidden or overlooked. Fatigue, lack of concentration, irritability, nervousness, and anger are signs of stress that can be easily dismissed as transitory and momentary— only to find later that they have festered and evolved into a physiological manifestation such as an ulcer or recurring headache. Even then, these may be seen as personal weaknesses needing medical treatment rather than organizational problems needing restructuring of the work environment. An increase in tardiness, leave time, or resistance to change may also be an indication of intolerable levels of stress that need immediate attention.

While stress cannot be eliminated from the workplace, organizations can use a variety of techniques to deal with it.

- The human resource department should create and department managers should promote a sound employee assistance program that can be easily and confidentially accessed by employees facing emerging or troublesome issues.

- Managers can put job stress in perspective by insisting that workers not work through their breaks and lunch hours or take work home with them on a regular basis. If the workload is too high, the solution may be to add more staff or additional resources—not burn out the current staff. The human resource department can help managers understand what are reasonable workload expectations by researching the literature on workload standards and by conducting its own job audit.

- The human resource department can assist by hiring stress relief consultants who teach staff how to manage stress. Some approaches, such as meditation, regular exercise, massage, and healthy eating, along with its corollary, limiting the consumption of caffeine, nicotine, and alcohol, try to reduce physical aspects of stress. Good physical health is linked to good mental health. Other forms of stress relief, such as humor, singing, dancing, and hobbies, take the approach that good mental health leads to good physical health. These psychological methods distract workers from stress by giving them a sense of accomplishment and closure that may be missing from some public workplaces.

- Managers, with the assistance of personnel specialists, can restructure the workplace to reduce stress. For example, instead of having one front-counter worker to handle customer inquiries and complaints all day long, maybe the job should be shared with several other workers for different parts of the day. On a larger scale, the organizational climate and culture could be improved by hiring organizational development consultants. In most organizations, the human resource department has the responsibility to identify and recommend these consultants.

The failure to deal with stress in the workplace has health and safety repercussions not only for the individual employee affected, but the organization as a whole. It is more than an economic issue amounting to stress-induced medical bills—it also causes lost productivity, decreased responsiveness to change, and the inability to accomplish the organization's goals. It is more than an individual mental and/or physical health issue—it affects the security of the entire organization when stress is contagious or the stress leads to workplace violence.

WORKPLACE VIOLENCE

In today's organizations, violence in the workplace can be both the cause for disciplinary action and the result of an employee's reaction to how employee problems are handled. Department and human resource managers share the responsibility for ensuring that all employees enjoy a safe and nonviolent work environment.

Workplace violence can take many forms, ranging from verbal threats, harassment, and intimidation to physical forms, such as pushing, slapping, sexual assault, kicking, and attacking with lethal weapons. It may also involve destruction of property (wasting resources, vandalism, and so on) and sabotage (setting off computer viruses, tampering with databases, mocking others behind their backs, or spreading rumors).

WORKPLACE VIOLENCE SURVEYS

The SHRM 1999 Workplace Violence Survey reported that 57 percent of survey respondents said that a violent incident had occurred in their workplace in 1999 compared to 48 percent in 1996.[9] Contrary to images presented in the media, the survey found that only 2 percent of workplace violence stems from shootings and stabbings.

More common acts of violence reported by respondents included verbal threats (41 percent) and pushing and shoving (19 percent). Personality conflicts were reported as the impetus for violent acts at work in 55 percent of incidents. Other common motivations included family or marital problems (36 percent) and work-related stress (24 percent).[10]

In the private sector, taxi drivers, hotel clerks, mini-mart clerks, and gas station attendants were the most likely victims because they work alone at night and have money or valued items that can be easily exchanged for money.[11] Not so surprisingly, in the public sector, police, medical professionals, social workers, and others who work with patients, clients, or customers known to have a history of violence or assault and to exhibit intimidating or belligerent behavior are more likely to be the victims of workplace homicide or nonfatal assaults. Managers and human resource specialists are vulnerable to these types of assaults because they are responsible for personnel actions that cause anger, frustration, and stress—selection, promotion, disciplinary actions, terminations, and conflict mediation.

WARNING SIGNS

What may be troubling to the average worker is not so much the frequency of violence in the workplace as the unpredictability of workplace victimization. Attempts to profile the typical perpetrator and identify the causes of workplace violence suggest that employees who have not been violent previously can be prone to fits of aggression and that, given the right circumstances, anyone could become violent in some form or fashion. Factors in these occurrences range from personal issues to work-related issues to societal issues, and there is much disagreement about the root causes. More recently, attention has been drawn to domestic violence as a potential cause of workplace violence. The danger stems from two concerns. First, domestic violence is vastly underreported and therefore is much more prevalent than we think. And second, the emotional turmoil of domestic violence has few boundaries and can easily spill over from the home to the workplace.

Indicators of increased risk of violent employee behavior include the following:

- direct or veiled threats of harm;
- intimidating, belligerent, harassing, bullying, or other inappropriate and aggressive behavior;
- numerous conflicts with supervisors and other employees;
- bringing a weapon to the workplace, brandishing a weapon in the workplace, making inappropriate references to guns, or fascination with weapons;
- statements showing fascination with incidents of workplace violence, statements indicating approval of the use of violence to resolve a problem, or statements indicating identification with perpetrators of workplace homicides;
- statements indicating desperation (over family, financial, and other personal problems) to the point of attempting suicide;
- drug/alcohol abuse; and
- extreme changes in behaviors.[12]

These behaviors should not be ignored since they are signs that an employee is potentially volatile. Managers may be able to avert some workplace violence by recognizing and dealing with employees' problems promptly.

PREVENTIVE MEASURES

What seem to be working to stem the tide of violence in the workplace are strong preventive measures. Managers and personnel specialists can work together to accomplish the following:

- Create an environment of mutual respect. Treat employees fairly and respectfully and they will treat you the same. Treating everyone fairly and with respect is a powerful agent to prevent increasing anger and a sense of powerlessness.

- Create an organizational culture that encourages open communications.

- Establish a zero tolerance policy toward violence in the workplace and be firm and consistent in applying it. Because verbal threats and harassment can escalate, they should be dealt with as quickly and as seriously as physical forms of violence are. Employees should sign an agreement acknowledging that they have read the policy and understand the consequences of violating it. The policy should be contained in standard operating procedures, referred to in training programs, and posted in prominent locations.

- Make the workplace as safe as possible by investing in appropriate security measures. At a minimum, work areas should be locked, employees should have ID badges, unauthorized persons should have limited access, and there should be a plan to deal with potential threats. Security guards, surveillance cameras, metal detectors, alarm systems, bulletproof walls and glass, and so forth may be appropriate in some public facilities. Security measures do not have to be elaborate or expensive. One of the less expensive methods is to encourage employees to report suspicious or unusual behavior.

- Develop a reasonable grievance process. This prevents grievants from believing that they have been wronged. An ineffective grievance process only creates more hostility and a sense of powerlessness. A functional grievance system allows grievants to vent, grieve, and find resolution to the conflict even if it is not in their favor.

- Protect potential targets. If a high-risk individual has been dismissed, the work schedule, break times, and staff meetings of affected parties should be immediately changed.

- Screen job applicants for a history of violence. A thorough background investigation that includes all forms of violence, even domestic violence, is needed.

- Create a joint management-employee committee to examine high-risk factors in the workplace, such as the types of patients, clients, or customers involved in previous incidents, the pattern of time, day, or location of violence, and the motives for past cases.

- Maintain an effective Employee Assistance Program (EAP) that can address issues that lead to workplace violence. The program should also be capable of dealing with the physical and psychological trauma suffered by victims of violence in the workplace.

WORKSHOP 6

Employee Safety and Health

PRE-SERVICE OR IN-SERVICE STUDENTS

Identifying Safety and Health Hazards

The purpose of this exercise is to increase student awareness of safety and health issues, especially hazards that are easily overlooked.

Instructions:

- Have students work independently to gather safety and health hazard information about an occupation.
- Assign students to groups wherein individual group members have investigated the same or similar occupations.
- Have students compare findings.

Research:

- Library research: Read and gather information about the safety and health hazards associated with a particular occupation. Universities with a government documents section may provide useful reports on investigations into selected occupations and industries.
- Field research (optional): Visit a work site to identify potential safety and health hazards. Locate the material safety data sheets and research the effects of the biohazardous chemicals and substances listed.
- Nonworking students: Do library research on household safety and health. Conduct a thorough investigation of the safety and health hazards in your own home/apartment. Be sure to investigate the medicine cabinet, any shelves under the kitchen sink, and the garage.

Group Discussion:

1. What are the top three safety hazards? Why are they important? What can be done to improve safety awareness?

2. What are the top three health hazards? What makes them so danger-ous? What are the appropriate prevention strategies?

3. How can department managers and personnel specialists work to-gether to reduce the impact of work-related injuries and illness?

Classroom Discussion:

1. What are the major safety and health issues?

2. What are the roles of department managers and the human resource department in reducing workers' compensation claims?

PRE-SERVICE OR IN-SERVICE STUDENTS

The Administration of Occupational Safety and Health Programs

As a result of this exercise, students will have an increased awareness of various public sector safety and health programs.

Format:

Students are randomly assigned to a work group. The instructor assigns each work group a research topic, such as

- What is risk management?
- What is self-insurance?
- What does your state OSHA do?
- What are the programs of the federal OSHA?
- What does the OSHRC do?
- What have been recent recommendations of NIOSH?
- How are effective management-worker safety committees built?
- What are workers entitled to under the prevailing right-to-know provisions?
- Are drug-testing policies a violation of an employee's civil rights?

Have groups present their findings to the class.

NOTES

1. Brent M. Giddens and Weston A. Edwards, "Communicable Diseases in the Work-place: How to Handle the Risks," SHRM White Paper [database online] (Alexandria, VA: SHRM, March 1999 [cited 24 March 2000]), member-restricted access from http://www.shrm.org.

2. Ibid.

3. Ibid.

4. "Sample Policy on AIDS," SHRM White Paper [database online] (Alexandria, VA: SHRM, July 1999 [cited 24 March 2000]), member-restricted access from http://www.shrm.org.

5. Ibid.

6. Ibid.

7. "Make Sure Your Policy's Not a Smoking Gun," in IPMA [database online] (Alexandria, VA: IPMA [cited 8 March 2000]), member-restricted access from http://www .ipma-hr.org.

8. Ibid.

9. "Workplace Violence Continues to Rise," *HR News Online,* in Society for Human Resource Management [database online] (Alexandria, VA: SHRM, 2 November 1999 [cited 13 March 2000]), member-restricted access at http://www.shrm.org.

10. Ibid.

11. National Institute for Occupational Safety and Health, *Violence in the Workplace: Risk Factors and Prevention Strategies,* Current Intelligence Bulletin 57, DHHS (NIOSH) Publication no. 96–100, 1996. Also available at http://www.cdc.gove/niosh/violhomi.html.

12. "Dealing with Workplace Violence: A Guide for Agency Planners—Part I: Section 1" [online] available from http://www.opm.gov/workplac/handbook/p1–s3.htm; accessed 8 March 2000.

7

WORKPLACE ETHICS

Effective department and human resource management depends upon people with ethics and integrity. Declaring that employees should be treated fairly and equally is a lot easier in theory than in practice. By their very nature, questions of ethics are very difficult to answer. Ethical questions take time to think through, and managers have precious little time. They require a clear sense of personal and societal values, which, to say the least, is difficult to achieve. Indeed, what is right or wrong, good or bad, about a managerial decision depends to a large extent upon what ethical and moral principles are taken into consideration, what values we hold important, who we think might be directly or indirectly affected by the decision, and what price we are willing to pay for our decision. One teacher of ethics and leadership aptly depicts the relationship between ethics and moral principles this way:

> Ethics is constituted by a set of normative prescriptions, against which we might evaluate, for example, the workplace behavior of human resource and department managers. Although these standards must be consistent with and, in some cases, derived from deeper moral principles, the two are not identical. Ethical standards are grounded in more substantive moral systems. Ethics attempts to draw upon the most generalizable parts of morality. In so doing, perhaps, it allows people with diverse commitments to work together in an environment structured by normative imperatives.[1]

Needless to say, the quality of ethical decision making depends upon both the moral character and vision of the decision maker. Although ethics is a frequent topic of the media and most states have statutes dealing with some aspect of ethical conduct,[2] most managers and human resource specialists have received little training in dealing with ethics. Often unethical behaviors result from ignorance rather than from malice. When a company or department provides the employees with clear explanations of moral and ethical standards, the employees are much more likely to meet such expectations.[3]

While this chapter will help department heads and human resource managers begin to sort out the issues that must be considered in creating an ethical work environment, it cannot provide a sure guide to morality or integrity. However, employees expect that human resource and department managers set and comply with ethical standards of behavior.

BOUNDARIES

THE LAW

There are statutes, codes of ethics, and administrative rules that define the proper roles and conduct of the manager and human resource administrator as well as the sanctions for improper behavior. As discussed in earlier chapters, several laws such as the Equal Pay Act of 1963, Civil Rights Act of 1991, and Americans with Disabilities Act of 1990 make it illegal to treat applicants, job incumbents, and promotional candidates differently in recruitment, selection, retention, and promotional activities. Because the law is constantly being interpreted and reinterpreted by the court system as new human resource situations arise, managers have a responsibility to ensure that they and their staff are trained in the various legal requirements of their jobs. Ignorance of the law is no defense.

While a public administrator's legal obligations are important, many of the situations that managers face on a day-to-day basis may not appear to be violations of known legal requirements. More important, the manager's role cannot be defined solely in legalistic terms.

Merely complying with rules and precedents is a very limited endeavor.

> Compliance programs exist to tell employees about the law and to prevent violations of law. Employees are motivated to do the right thing by a fear of being caught, but such programs . . . rarely help employees resolve those situations involving right and wrong that are not covered by the law. Organizations must develop the ethical commitment and expertise of their employees.[4]

For example, most governmental organizations have internal codes of ethics, administrative rules, and statutes requiring the disclosure of conflict of interest. Thus, a purchasing agent who receives a free gift for buying products from a particular vendor must report the gift if it exceeds a specified amount. Although a common practice in the private sector, this is considered illegal in the public sector because it can lead to corruption and because it gives the appearance of impropriety. But what if the vendor sends the purchasing agent no single gift that exceeds the legal limit, but the total value of all of the gifts is considerable? What if the gift is not a personal gift, such as an offer to sponsor the purchasing agent's child's soccer team? What if the gift has no significant monetary value, but has considerable symbolic value (such as nomination to the local Rotary Club)? What if the purchasing agent reports and/or returns the gift(s) and chooses to have a casual friendship with the vendor? And what if there has been no exchange of gifts and no apparent unfair practices, but the purchasing agent is a member of the same religious organization as the vendor or an employee of the vendor? These are situations that statutory conflict of interest laws may not address and now fall upon the manager to resolve.

SEXUAL HARASSMENT

Sexual harassment is another major area of concern in the workforce. It is considered to exist when unwelcome sexual advances persist, a hostile work environment exists, or requests for sexual favors are made a condition for employment or promotion. Sexual harassment includes situations involving men and women as well as same-sex offenses by supervisors, coworkers, and nonemployees such as contractors at the work site. Under the Title VII prohibition against sex discrimination, employers are required to develop and distribute sexual harassment policies, to take immediate action to investigate, to resolve complaints in this area, and to take care that they do not retaliate against the complainant.[5] In addition, employers are responsible for taking disciplinary action against employees who are known to have sexually harassed a subordinate or coworkers, since employment discrimination laws also apply to harassment by nonsupervisory workers. In some organizations, the penalty for any form of workplace discrimination may be termination.

For department and human resource managers, the most difficult aspect of enforcing antisexual harassment policies is that a number of complaints are not always clear-cut and fall into gray areas. There are no instructions that identify the various forms of sexual harassment and show managers how to proceed in each case. However, there are some basic guidelines that can assist department and human resource managers.

HUMAN RESOURCE DEPARTMENT:
- Develop a clear policy that defines and prohibits sexual harassment.
- Distribute your policy and make sure that all employees sign an acknowledgment of receipt of the policy.
- Train supervisors on how to handle complaints.
- Make sure employees and supervisors know that retaliation will not be tolerated.

DEPARTMENT MANAGERS:
- Listen to your employees.
- Investigate every complaint and follow your policy for each complaint.
- Follow up with the employee to make sure the harassment has stopped and that no retaliation has taken place.[6]

WORKPLACE DATING

One problem that managers find in implementing antisexual harassment policies is the confusion between sexual harassment and workplace dating or romances. With more men and women working together than ever, workplace romances are increasing. A 1994 American Management Association (AMA) survey reported that more than 30 percent of employees said that they had dated a coworker during their career; and a 1998 Love@Work survey stated that 71 percent of the seven thousand respondents reported dating at work, and 50 percent of the managers acknowledged having dated a person they supervised.[7]

Though some positive results have been expressed concerning workplace romance, such as increased motivation, creativity, and productivity on the job, many problems can and do result. Department and human resource managers fear repercussions such as accusations of favoritism, conflict of interest, lower coworker morale, retaliation at the end of a romance, and claims of sexual harassment.[8] Due to these problems, workplace romance policies are beginning to emerge in some organizations. A 1997 IPMA survey stated that 3 percent of the 345 participating government agencies had written policies on workplace dating and 13 percent of companies surveyed by the Society for Human Resource Management (SHRM) had written policies.[9]

The purpose of developing written polices on workplace romance is to create guidelines that managers can apply fairly and consistently. Some organizations allow voluntary disclosure of consensual relationships while others require disclosure in order to monitor inappropriate use of authority and reduce claims of sexual harassment later. Regardless of the approach that the organization takes, several basic guidelines should be considered with regard to workplace dating or romance.

- Put the policy in writing and distribute it to all current and new employees.
- Hold question-and-answer sessions to allow supervisors to gain clarity concerning the policy.
- Make sure that the policy applies to all close relationships between coworkers regardless of marital status.
- Once the relationship is disclosed to the supervisor, make sure that the information remains confidential.
- Coworkers involved in close personal relationships should be prohibited from working in supervisor/subordinate roles. In these cases, a transfer may be arranged for one of the employees, or in small organizations, performance appraisals and other employment decisions should involve input from another supervisor or manager.
- Require employees to refrain from public displays of affection and extensive conversation.
- Make sure that the policy applies to all employees, including senior managers and executives.
- Obtain a legal review to assure compliance with federal, state, and local laws.[10]

THE PROFESSION

Some professions have stringent expectations for their members, often expressed in the profession's code of ethics and/or professional standards of conduct. Members who are charged with violating these codes and standards are given a quasi-judicial hearing that follows the profession's due process procedures and rules of evidence. At stake are the member's professional reputation and ability to remain in the profession. Thus, social workers who violate a client's confidentiality or who have intimate relations with their clients may be penalized by dismissal from the profession.

Just like the legal requirements for one's job, professional codes of ethics and rules of conduct do not cover every conceivable human act. Moreover, critics express concern that professionals monitoring other professionals is equivalent to the fox watching the henhouse, since to find against one's peer is to find fault with and bring dishonor upon the profession's educational system, self-monitoring capability, disinterested neutrality, and sworn allegiance to uphold the public interest as a public trust. Further, in the case of the errant social worker, while she/he may be expelled from the National Association of Social Workers (NASW), she/he may continue to engage in counseling in many states because not all social workers are members of NASW. Similarly, a doctor who has been punished in one state may move to another state and establish a new practice because there is no national sanctioning body, but rather fifty independent state medical boards. National organizations, such as the American Medical Association and American Bar Association, endorse model codes of ethics and professional standards, but leave the administration of these devices to states.

To complicate matters further, while many occupations think of themselves as being professional, to the point of having a published code of ethics, most professions are not true professions. The IPMA, for example, has some of the characteristics of a profession: a body of knowledge, an organization that supports identification of the profession as unique and of benefit to society, and a code of ethics. However, its code of ethics (see Appendix C) is more aspirational and inspirational than a guide for professional conduct or basis for sanctioning members. There is no accrediting body that controls the curriculum that human resource specialists must receive to become competent in the field. There is no required certification process that mandates members to pass a written examination, intern under the watchful eye of a seasoned professional, or gain experience in an accredited organization, and there are no state boards or commissions that license all human resource managers. There is, however, a highly recognized voluntary Professional in Human Resource (PHR) and Senior Professional in Human Resource (SPHR) certification process that is administered through the SHRM. Increasingly, public sector organizations require the certification as a qualification prerequisite for their human resource specialists' and managers' positions.

Human resource and department managers should still join the society, association, or organization that most represents their professional expertise and interests. By having trained professionals administering the human resource and department functions, there will be greater consistency in accepted practices and ethics in the profession. Major public sector associations such as the American Society for Public Administration (ASPA) provide a greater commonality in how organizations are run and what the ethical standards are in public management. In addition, the National Association of Schools of Public Administration and Affairs (NASPAA) sets the accreditation standards for masters' programs in public administration.

THE ORGANIZATION'S MISSION

Regardless of whether one is a member of a profession or not, the fact that most people are not independent professionals but employees of an organization creates its own set of ethical issues. For example, an accountant discovers that proper accounting procedures are not being followed. Being loyal to the organization, the accountant reports the problem through the chain of command. However, executive managers are concerned about the practice being disclosed because the adverse publicity might jeopardize the organization's standing. The remedy that is proposed only compounds the duplicity. While there are laws that protect an employee from being ordered to commit an illegal act, it is often difficult to discern when, and if, an order is inappropriate. What is the right course for the accountant to take—to risk breaching confidentiality and take this to the accounting professional community for advice, to become "an anonymous source" and leak this to the news media, or to simply follow orders since the organization is paying the accountant's salary and is assuming responsibility for the order?

Beyond the question of whether professionals should be true first to their profession or to the organization is determination of the extent to which organizational norms promote fairness and equality while not conflicting with other normative standards. The organization's mission drives the goals and objectives for organizational units and members. Because mission statements usually are also statements about management philosophy, they define many organizational norms, such as being responsive to customer needs, treating all employees and customers fairly and equally, or promoting efficiency wherever and whenever possible. While these may appear to be logical and clear upon first reading, their application may be problematic. For example, while efficiency is important, being responsive to one patron's needs may mean unequal treatment and ignoring the needs of the next customer. However, to be efficient and handle every customer quickly and with the same treatment may be unresponsive if not disrespectful since members of the public have diverse needs.

Defining the goals of one's department or human resource function by the organization's mission may also present its own set of problems. For example, let us say that the mission of a public organization includes an ethical commitment to require that its employment policies and practices are nondiscriminatory and that its workforce is representative of the public it serves. The satisfaction with responsiveness to the public's expectations of ethical standards, of course, depends upon where one sits. Some white males seek changes in hiring and promotional practices because of perceptions of reverse discrimination while women and minorities seek changes in practices that they believe adversely affect them. Each thinks the other has unfair advantages, and all expect the organization to be responsive to their needs. How should department and human resource managers carry out the mission statement in view of these disparate concerns?

If the organization's mission defines its purpose and values, does it also define the values of the individual employee? That is, does an organization have a right to expect its employees to subordinate their values to the employer? Most human resource departments can cite laws, such as the Hatch Act of 1939, that restrict public sector career employees' political activities, and most have administrative rules about outside activities. For example, a moonlighting employee may not engage in activities that directly or indirectly damage the reputation of the employer. But there are also many gray areas not covered by existing policy and procedures. For example, recent medical research indicates that tissue from aborted fetuses may offer hope for forestalling or remedying the effects of Alzheimer's disease. Does the Department of Health and Human Services (DHHS) have the right to expect its employees who oppose abortion to support its policy to investigate the efficacy of this treatment? Does DHHS have an obligation to allow worker input into what its public policy should be? Can it allow some workers to opt out of following the agency's directives?

In spite of the confusion that an agency's mission can bring, it also defines to a certain extent the scope of management's authority over its workers. Those work activities that fall within the scope of the mission are clearly within the purview of managers. Those outside the boundaries will need discussion and negotiation.

THE POLITICAL ENVIRONMENT

The public also has expectations about its public servants. As indicated in Chapter 1, the public has come to have high standards for its employees. The Washingtonian era created a demand for people loyal to this country, educated, and of impeccable character. The Jacksonian era emphasized the need for public servants to be responsive to and represent us all. The passage of the Pendleton Act in 1883 heightened public distaste for corruption and even the appearance of impropriety.

These expectations, however, do not come without a cost. The alleged and confirmed sexual escapades of various presidents have caused political commentators and the press to examine the character issue in both the public and private lives of public figures. Such scrutiny has a "spillover effect" in the lives of political appointees and high-ranking public administrators.

ETHICAL PRINCIPLES

There are common reoccurring ethical issues that are sources of frustration and skepticism among employees. Specific examples of these issues are included in Workshop 7 at the end of the chapter. The integrity of department and human resource managers is partly founded on the consistency with which they apply ethical principles or imperatives. These imperatives might be divided into three categories: administrative, philosophical, and personal.

ADMINISTRATIVE IMPERATIVES. Public administration has at least three competing imperatives.[11] The admonition to "do what is right" is the ideal. It suggests that managers should follow a principled approach no matter what the consequences. The errant accountant described earlier in the chapter may therefore decide to blow the whistle on the cover-up by her/his superiors in spite of the likelihood that she/he will be fired. However, a hard-and-fast principle, such as to never tell a lie, has its limits because lies are not always the dishonorable course of action. If by lying you could save the life of another, for instance, then this would be a noble lie. Seldom, however, will managers find a situation for lying that is so dramatically or obviously the right choice. Subtler circumstances demand careful consideration of alternatives to dishonesty.[12]

The space shuttle *Challenger* disaster provides a public sector example of a case involving major ethical decisions. In their zeal to save the space program, did National Aeronautics and Space Administration (NASA) managers adequately assess the dangers involved in the launch? How should the fact that they had never faced a comparable dilemma have influenced their decision making? Were they being truthful with themselves and others when they declared the shuttle safe to launch? Can they justify their action (or inaction) because they truly believed that the doomed astronauts were fully aware of the risks? Was their attempt to salvage the space program worth the risk?

Because "doing what is right" is not as simple as it first looks, many administrators follow the utilitarian approach—"do what will benefit the greatest number." Many American policy decisions are founded in this utilitarian imperative. The writings of Jeremy Bentham and John Stuart Mill argued strongly for the utilitarian point of view. To their way of thinking, ethical conduct was that which led to the greatest good for the greatest number. Hence, we condemn certain real estate property to make way for a highway because it benefits the larger community. Limited by resources, our domestic policy does not eliminate poverty for all, but targets the largest possible number of promising cases given the resources available. Making utilitarian choices is not easy, since one's preferences and calculations are always a point of contention for those with different formulae for fairness, effectiveness, and equality.

Finally, administrators may adopt a do-no-harm strategy. Many public policies are the result of this imperative because maintaining the political policy-making process is more important than the outcomes of these policies. Public policy making, after all, involves compromise, a necessary succession of decisions to preserve the ability to negotiate in the future.

PHILOSOPHICAL IMPERATIVES. Civic expectations regarding knowledge about ethics have their foundations in ancient Greece. Plato argued that individuals should be educated because it took incredible mental discipline to objectively define moral principles. He reasoned that no one would act immorally if he or she knew what the "good life" was. It would be illogical to act against one's own interest. Evil, to this way of thinking, results from lack of this knowledge. To Plato, moral principles were absolute; there were no exceptions. Whereas Plato thought in absolute terms about ethics, Aristotle believed in the "golden mean," the idea that an ethical life was to be lived in moderation, between two extremes. Hence, ethical behavior was not the same for everyone. Courage is to be found between the extremes of cowardice and rashness, but at a different point for different people in different circumstances. For Aristotle, what was ethical was relative to the situation. Whether one agrees with Plato or Aristotle, the tradition of thinking rationally about ethics and trying to deduce the moral significance of our actions remains with us today.

"Do unto others as you would have them do unto you" is a fundamental imperative that is found in several organized religions: Buddhism, Hinduism, Judaism, and Christianity. It is similar to Immanuel Kant's categorical imperative that suggests we live only by universal rules we would also want others to live by. From this concept emerges the idea that all should be treated as an end in themselves rather than as a means to someone else's end, since to treat others as a means to an end would, as a universal law, have us all treat each other poorly. These ideas remain with us today as a measuring stick for evaluating our efforts to be fair and impartial.

PERSONAL IMPERATIVES.   While most religions have a list of dos and don'ts to live by, most were not designed for the workplace as we know it today. Mary Ellen Guy suggests that the acronym CHAPELFIRZ contains important moral values that should guide a manager's ethical decision making.[13] CHAPELFIRZ stands for Caring, Honesty, Accountability, Promise keeping, pursuit of Excellence, Loyalty, Fairness, Integrity, Respect for others, and responsible citiZenship. Organizations do not function well if responsible citizenship, pursuit of excellence, and accountability are missing. Interpersonal relations suffer if there are not fairness, promise keeping, loyalty, caring for others, and respect for others. Personal decency begins with honesty and integrity.

ETHICAL DECISION MAKING

That the administrative, philosophical, and personal imperatives are not easily reconciled is not surprising. America is an amalgamation of heritages, ideologies, and cross-purposes. Moreover, ethics is a complex concept. While having earlier defined "integrity" as the consistency with which one applies ethical principles, integrity is but one part of what makes for an ethical administrator. An ethical manager must also be able to reason ethically.

Ethical reasoning can be said to follow the standard problem-solving model, but several special questions and perspectives augment it.

IDENTIFY THE PROBLEM

This is the most important element in the problem-solving process. Besides distinguishing between superficial and underlying problems, the ethical manager will want to ask what ethical principles and values are at stake, not just what rules and regulations were violated. Thus, a complaint about not receiving notice about a job opening should not focus solely on whether or not the job was properly posted, but may include questions about fairness (accessibility) and equity (should there have been a special effort to recruit targeted populations). If the ethical issues are beyond the grasp of the administrator, then perhaps an applied or business ethicist should be consulted to ensure that all ethical parameters are explored.

IDENTIFY THE ALTERNATIVES

Ethical decision making requires not only the identification of optional solutions but also a fair consideration of those who might be affected by the decision. If the Kantian categorical imperative is followed, then each stakeholder in the decision has value and his or her opinion counts. Typical administrative decision making, in contrast, looks at limited options and frequently focuses primarily on the benefit to management. In ethical decision making, any final solution cannot exclude employees as stakeholders because to do so would be to use them as means to an end. Open discussions with stakeholders may take time, but they will help ensure commitment and motivation to bring about a satisfactory resolution.

WEIGH THE CONSEQUENCES

The consequences must be measured against standards above and beyond the legal definition of what is permissible. In the ethical decision-making process, while the goal is to maximize critical values and uphold important principles, it is not unusual to find that several values and principles are in direct conflict with each other, or that the consequences affect different stakeholders in an uneven fashion. This is why many issues involving ethical behavior are referred to as ethical dilemmas. Guy suggests using CHAPELFIRZ as the model for cross-comparing consequences. In her book, she emphasizes applying these ten values to different ethical situations. Administrators concerned about understanding the consequences of their actions might begin by asking the stakeholders how the prospective options might relate to each of the CHAPELFIRZ values. These relationships could then be carefully considered, enabling the stakeholders and the administrator to reach a consensus on what is most important. Notice that the focus here is on prioritization of values and principles rather than ease of implementation, or the question of who will benefit.

Pick a Solution

The nature of ethical decision making is such that rarely does implementation depend solely upon managers. The implementation of ethical decisions often involves people who do not share the same values or principles, hence the involvement of additional stakeholders in the decision-making process.

There is also a big difference between implementation to the letter of the law and to the spirit of the law. The former, a minimalist view, runs the risk of destroying the credibility of the administrator, while the latter may meet with sharp resistance from the organizational status quo. If there has been open and honest communication among stakeholders, resistance to change should be minimal.

Hun-Joon Park proposes that essential to business ethics education is the "develop[ment] of moral imagination . . ." Optimally, a manager first comprehends the issues at stake and then considers the various precedents, but finally he or she "seek[s] ethical alternatives by which all stakeholders can justify their moral claims."[14] Rather than choose a solution from two unacceptable options (the lesser-of-two-evils approach), managers should seek new possibilities by creating a third ethical alternative.

Monitor and Evaluate

Measuring the outcomes may be difficult if the desire is to have statistics to compare. Qualitative measures may suffice, but more open-ended discussions among stakeholders may be more productive. Do not be surprised if there is an attempt to reopen the debate about what values and principles are at stake. While this may sound problematic to some, this is exactly what the ethical decision-making process is about. The establishment of a ethical community does not begin or end with a single decision, but is an ongoing process of compromise, consensus, moral imagination, and renewal.

GUIDELINES

While not necessarily complete, the following serve as a general road map for thinking and acting ethically. While it may be difficult to see the ethical quandaries in the humdrum of daily routines, following these guidelines can reduce or prevent ethical dilemmas.

1. Keep an open mind. People do not always share the same values or principles about ethical conduct. Ethical decision making is as much about inquiring into what motivates behavior as it is about reaching a conclusion.

2. Think broadly. Ethics is more than what is legally required. It involves questions about fairness, equity, and justice, not just organizational

efficiency and effectiveness. Think about the meaning of decisions and actions for humankind, not just the situation at hand.

3. Set high personal ethical standards. Integrity is based upon your deeds, not just your words. The courage of one's convictions can be lost in a moment's hesitation or self-doubt. Effective leadership is difficult for a person with questionable ethics.

4. When unethical conduct is discovered, take corrective action. Failure to take action sends the wrong message. Indecision implies that the unethical behavior is to be condoned.

5. Be consistent. In ethics there are sometimes more exceptions than rules. Appreciating mitigating circumstances should not be to the detriment of the underlying precepts. If much thought is given to the reason behind the exception, one may discover that it is based upon a competing value or principle. Thus, being consistent also means knowing the priority of one's values.

6. Involve stakeholders in the decision-making process. Even though this is time-consuming, the benefits outweigh the costs. When stakeholders build a moral community, the responsibility is shared and the obligations are mutual.

In the end, there is no easy way to become an ethical public manager or personnel specialist. It requires a great deal of thought and analysis followed by consistent actions that confront unethical behavior. There are no hard-and-fast rules to follow because an ethical approach is based upon a thorough examination of competing claims and principles.

WORKSHOP 7

Ethics and Ethical Choices

PRE-SERVICE STUDENTS

Part I—Ethical Decision Making

Instructions:

Prior to this workshop, students should gather information about race relations, equal employment opportunity, affirmative action, and California Proposition 209. Half of the students should argue for Proposition 209; half against. Each group should be reflective of the diversity present. For additional personal growth and insight, students may wish to be on the side opposite to their own beliefs.

Preparation:

What are the essential administrative, human resource, and human principles at stake for/against affirmative action? Who are the stakeholders and
what rights of theirs must be protected in this debate? What is the mission
of a human resource department vis-à-vis equal employment opportunity
and social equity?

What elements of CHAPELFIRZ are supported by your position on 209?
Prepare to argue why your position reinforces "do no harm," "greatest good
for the greatest number," or "doing what is right." Explain how your position is not self-interested.

Debate:

The following question is to be debated:

California voters have overwhelmingly passed Proposition 209 outlawing affirmative action in hiring and promotion of workers. However, a court injunction
has temporarily stopped the enactment of 209. Your organization receives federal financial assistance and therefore must have an affirmative action plan. What
should your human resource department's policies be (1) until 209 is out of the
court system, and (2) if 209 finally becomes law?

Each side is given fifteen minutes to present its argument without interrup-
tion. After both sides have presented, each has ten minutes for rebuttal. Alternating between sides for the next fifteen minutes, allow each side to ask
questions of their opponents.

Feedback:

After a brief break, the entire group should critique their own presentation
and discuss their reactions to their opponents' presentation. As one group,
how would they work together to build a moral community that treats its
members fairly and equally, yet allows for special treatment of those who
had been previously excluded from participating? What difference would
it make if the prior exclusion were deliberate? Inadvertent?

Part 2—Ethical Values

Instructions:

The goal of this workshop is to explore the values and principles underlying various human resource issues. Students should work in small groups
so that these values can be identified and prioritized.

Group Activity:

Select a situation from the human resource situations listed below. What
are the values that underlie the situation? Who are the major and secondary

stakeholders? How are they affected by the situation? What might the ethical basis for their position be?

- Describe a management policy that would meet the letter of the law. Describe a management policy that would maximize important values/principles. How might the stakeholders respond to the implementation of each policy?
- Using the CHAPELFIRZ model, evaluate the relationship of your preferred policy to the ten values.
- Report your findings to the larger group. Compare and contrast the different values/principles involved. Discuss the differences in priorities.

List of Human Resource Situations:

1. Preselection. A manager knows whom he or she wants and tells you whom to hire before the selection process has begun. This is common practice for key executive positions because people who can be trusted are needed.

2. Most organizations have rules prohibiting the use of government equipment for personal purposes. However, most workers regularly phone their loved ones, "borrow" a pen or two, and photocopy a few personal items. The rationales are that everyone does it; it makes up for low pay, uncompensated use of personal resources, and overtime worked; and the impact is minuscule in a multi-million-dollar budget. Your fellow supervisors say to ignore it and want you to remain silent.

3. A manager puts in a reclassification for a loyal employee. It becomes obvious that this employee has few new job duties justifying a reallocation. The manager pressures you to grant the reclassification because she/he is fearful of losing the employee. (Option A: The manager argues that this is the customary method for rewarding outstanding performance and cites numerous instances granted by your predecessor. Option B: The manager explains that the employee has fallen upon hard economic times because his wife had to quit her job because their new baby needs expensive cancer treatment.)

4. Jobs are hard to find. The human resource analyst responsible for selection has been giving high scores to his/her friends and relatives. Because this is not your area, you cannot fully investigate it. You wish to tell the human resource director, but the errant analyst will immediately know who made the complaint. (Option A: There are few applicants for the position. Option B: There are many applicants for the position. Option C: The human resource director is the analyst's mentor.)

5. Minorities, women, immigrants, and disabled people are often difficult to recruit and retain. Managers also may be reluctant to manage in their normal manner because discrimination statutes protect individuals in

these groups. Your manager has told you not to hire individuals from protected categories, not because they are unqualified, but because she/he believes they are a liability in the long run. Failure to follow the order will likely lead to repercussions.

6. John has been disciplined in the past for making suggestive remarks to the young women in his office. He is an older man who rationalized his conduct as expressions of interpersonal (not sexual) caring and joking. He has now learned that he can avoid further discipline by obeying the letter of the law. If a female employee objects to being called "sweetie," he stops, but then uses a never-ending repertoire of other endearing, diminutive terms until the victim gives up. No new complaints have been filed in the past two years. You want to tell the next new secretary about John.

7. A coworker, for some unknown reason, has hassled you since you began working in the organization. You accidentally run across a memorandum that contains information that she/he could use. If this were a friend, you might share the information because you know the source would be held in confidence. Since the coworker is not a friend, you could destroy the memorandum and no one would know. (Option A: The information could lead to recognition and reward for the coworker. Option B: Disclosing the information would further the interests of the entire work group. Option C: Disclosing the information to the right people would destroy your rival.)

8. Parents often find themselves selling candy at work in order for their child to participate in organized sports. You have bought your share of "goodies," and it is a common practice in the office in spite of rules to the contrary. It has come to your attention as manager that one of your supervisors is taking advantage of his/her authority to unduly pressure subordinates to buy candy so his/her child can remain the top-selling student in the region.

9. A worker under your direction has come up with a superior idea. You give the worker an outstanding performance evaluation as a reward. To upper managers, however, you represent the idea as your own. Your reasoning: The idea would not have come about without your initial direction and allocation of resources, and you are in a better position to utilize the organizational rewards because you plan to improve your entire unit's standing as a result; legally, all work products produced on government time and with government resources belong to the government.

10. Asbestos ceiling tiles were a common fixture in buildings built thirty or more years ago. However, research indicates that exposure to asbestos particles causes potentially fatal lung disease. Your organization has chosen to hide the tile underneath a false dropped ceiling. OSHA requires that employers notify workers of environmental hazards. For some reason, your predecessors have never listed this hazard. So far no

one has gotten sick. Asbestos eradication would be expensive since the building would have to be evacuated for several months and special handling required. Disclosure would likely bring the agency budget to a halt, eliminating programs for your clients, the poor, and the elderly.

11. A grievance has been filed against you. The union representative stops by to informally discuss the grievance. You deliberately lie to the union representative about the incident. The union representative will never know that you lied and the grievance will end. (Option A: You justify your actions on the basis of the worker's having been dishonest with you. Option B: You reason that you have sufficient proof of unsatisfactory performance in other areas to get rid of the malcontent. Option C: The grievance is clearly unfounded and meant to harass you. Option D: The grievance is valid. Option E: You are undergoing a great deal of stress because a loved one has died recently and you don't want to add to your stress level.)

IN-SERVICE STUDENTS

Ethical Decision Making

Preview the video *A Major Malfunction: The Story behind the Space Shuttle Challenger Disaster.*[15] In groups of four or five, identify and discuss the major ethical problems involved in this case. Answer the questions in the chapter about the *Challenger* disaster.

- In their zeal to save the space program, did NASA managers adequately assess the dangers involved in the launch?
- How should the fact that they had never faced a comparable dilemma have influenced their decision making?
- Were they being truthful with themselves and others when they declared the shuttle safe to launch?
- Can they justify their action (or inaction) because they truly believed that the doomed astronauts were fully aware of the risks?
- Was their attempt to salvage the space program worth the risk?

Ask group members to provide cases or examples from their public sector experiences or observations that illustrate ethical decision-making dilemmas. Discuss the ethical solutions that decision makers could have used in each case.

Notes

1. Terry Price, e-mail message to the author, 20 March 2000.

2. Carol W. Lewis, *The Ethics Challenge in Public Service* (San Francisco: Jossey-Bass, 1991), 17.

3. Randi L. Sims and Thomas L. Leon, "The Influence of Organizational Expectations on Ethical Decision-Making Conflict," *The Journal of Business Ethics* 23 (2000): 220.

4. Dawn-Marie Driscoll, W. Michael Hoffman, and Joseph E. Murphy, "Business Ethics and Compliance: What Management Is Doing and Why," *Business and Society Review 99* (fall 1996): 40.

5. U.S. Equal Employment Opportunity Commission, "Federal Laws Prohibiting Job Discrimination: Questions and Answers" (Washington, DC, December 1998) [online] Available from http://www.eeoc.gov/facts/qanda.html.

6. "An Employer's Guide to an Anti-sexual Harassment Plan," in IPMA [database online] (Alexandria, VA: IPMA [cited 8 March 2000]), member-restricted access at http://www.ipma-hr.org.

7. Joe Lustig, "Dating in the Workplace," in IPMA [database online] (Alexandria, VA: IPMA [cited 8 March 2000]), member-restricted access at http://www.ipma-hr.org.

8. Ibid.

9. Ibid.

10. Ibid.

11. For an in-depth discussion, see Dalton S. Lee, "The Difficulty with Ethics Education in Public Administration," *International Journal of Public Administration* 13 (1 & 2): 181–205 (1990).

12. Peter M. Leitner and Ronald J. Stupak, "Ethics, National Security and Bureaucratic Reality: North Knight and Designated Liars," *American Review of Public Administration* 27 (1): 69 (1997).

13. Mary Ellen Guy, *Ethical Decision Making in Everyday Work Situations* (New York: Quorum Books, 1990): 15–17. For a more recent model of ethics developed specifically for academic environments, see Deborah S. Keliner and Mary D. Maury, "Thou Shalt and Shalt Not: An Alternative to the Ten Commandments Approach to Developing a Code of Ethics for Schools of Business," *Journal of Business Ethics* 16 (1997): 331–336.

14. Hun-Joon Park, "Can Business Ethics Be Taught? A New Model of Business Ethics Education," *Journal of Business Ethics* 17 (9/10): 970 (1998).

15. *A Major Malfunction: The Story behind the Space Shuttle Challenger Disaster,* dir. Mark Maier, 161 min., Research Foundation of the State University, Binghamton, NY, 1992, videocassette.

8

THE NEW MILLENNIUM WORKPLACE

DEMOGRAPHIC TRENDS

In the new millennium, we have the opportunity to discard unworkable human management systems developed over the past century and to outfit ourselves with successful and fresh ideas for the future. "Participation," "empowerment," "teams," "virtual workplaces." These words, seldom heard in the organizations of the 1950s and 1960s, may well define the spirit of twenty-first-century organizations.

New millennium workers differ from their predecessors in significant ways. We know from the media and government reports that the workplace will continue to become more diverse. The largest group of new entrants into the workforce comprises women, immigrants, and people of color while a substantial portion of the current employees are older workers. The Department of Labor (DOL) reports the following:

- By 2050, the U.S. population is expected to increase by 50 percent, and minority groups will make up nearly half the population.
- Immigration will account for almost two-thirds of the nation's population growth.
- The population of older Americans is expected to more than double.
- One-quarter of all Americans will be of Hispanic origin.
- Almost one in ten Americans will be of Asian or Pacific Islander descent.
- More women and people with disabilities will be on the job.[1]

The percentage of women in the workforce is rising while participation by men is declining. Since 1967, the percentage of working women has grown from 41 percent to 60 percent (though this growth is expected to level off) compared to a decrease for male workers from 80 percent to 75 percent.[2] Three of every four women with children are in the workforce.

Educational levels are increasing along with a concurrent rise in the demand from employers for highly educated and skilled workers. Specialized technology workers are at a premium while many other entrants into the workforce do not possess adequate skills to be competitive or to advance. Added to this reality is the fact that large numbers of baby boomers with education, skills, and experience will retire in the next ten years.

Based on these factors, the *Futurework* report raises a number of essential questions for human resource and department managers. Some of the most compelling questions from the report clearly illustrate the complexity of these challenges.

■ How can we harness the resulting opportunities presented by increased diversity for economic growth? Does difference necessarily lead to discrimination? How can we get low-wage workers "unstuck" and into better-paying jobs?

■ How can we remove the multiple barriers that keep many of the poorest Americans from entering and then succeeding in the workforce—barriers such as low skills, discrimination, lack of transportation, lack of contacts in the labor market, and lack of child-care programs?

■ As computer networks compete with human networks in our workplaces, who will guide and mentor new workers on the job?

■ How can workers balance their needs for both lifelong economic security and the resources and time to care for their families?

■ Will policy makers and decision makers in government, labor unions, private industry, schools, and communities address the changes that are inevitable and embrace the challenge of meeting future workers' needs?

What options can human resource professionals offer department managers and employees to help them respond to these new and complex challenges?

Judy and D'Amico summarize the problems that are inherent in these questions and trends in "Workforce 2020."[3] They foresee a "bifurcated" vision for the U.S. workforce.

> As we envision the next twenty years, the skills premium appears even more powerful to us than it did to our predecessors who wrote "Workforce 2000." Millions of Americans with solid grounding in math, science and the English language will join a global elite whose services will be in intense demand. These workers will command generous and growing compensations. But other Americans with inadequate education and technological expertise—how many depends in large part on what we do to improve their training—will face declining real wages. Wise macro-economic policy and burgeoning local markets for goods and services in some parts of the U.S. will stave off large-scale unemployment and dependency, but too high a rate of unskilled to skilled workers in the American workforce will lead to a further division of the American society into haves and have-nots.[4]

CAPACITY BUILDING

Capacity building refers to the development of human competence, capabilities, and qualifications to meet the needs of society and the workplace. Building human capacity to meet the growing needs of the information society is complex on several levels. Richard Judy indicates that in today's workplace, "skills requirements of the occupations that are growing in numbers are much higher than those of the occupations that are actually shrinking."[5] These growing job categories require more advanced levels of language, math, and reasoning skills than the jobs that are declining. Since jobs with low skills requirements are disappearing, new entrants into the job market will need to invest longer periods of time in education and training prior to entering the workforce. Educational systems will need to increase their students' abilities and skills in the areas that employers require; and employers will need to offer more training and development programs to meet their human resource needs.

WORKFORCE DEVELOPMENT

Government programs and human resource managers are helping potential employees, including welfare-to-work participants, prepare for jobs before they enter the workplace in an effort to overcome the skills shortages that employers are experiencing. One such approach is the school-to-work program, which is a partnership between schools and employers to help youth develop the skills they need to make the transition from school to their first jobs.[6] These programs provide students with the opportunity to complete a sequence of courses in a particular field of work or postsecondary education and include work-based learning, school-based learning, and connected activities.[7]

For individuals who are no longer in school and need skills development or retraining, the Workforce Investment Partnership Act of 1998 provides training for positions that job seekers select from a list provided by local employers.[8] They choose a course that will provide the skills for the job using vouchers to pay the tuition. The intent of the program is to help job seekers gain training for jobs that are actually available and to provide employers with applicants who have the skills that their jobs require.[9]

Employers face different issues concerning workers who are already in the organization. Increasingly, employers are establishing "workplace education" programs to improve reading, writing, math, and other related skills.[10] A number of employees enter the workplace without some of the basic skills that are expected of a high school or vocational school graduate. These programs are needed as part of an overall training program, especially in organizations where they are adopting participatory programs, or implementing new technology or new training.[11]

CAREER DEVELOPMENT PROGRAMS

Career development programs help workers to identify a career path (lateral and vertical), specify the skills they will need to get there, and select the educational or training programs that will provide them with the knowledge and skills. Educational programs that are identified in these career development plans are often provided through tuition reimbursement, employer-paid advanced training and certificate programs, and on-site education programs. Such programs help public sector organizations retain highly skilled employees and lessen the need for job-hopping to gain better opportunities.

Many organizations use "core competencies" to assure that the employees' career development meets both the needs of employees and the agency. For example, the Leadership Program in Henrico County, Virginia, identified twenty competencies that contribute to the success of progressive organizations. During one year the program focused on the enhancement of competencies in employee development and coaching, technological literacy, team leadership and empowerment, strategic management, organizational astuteness, and orientation to the future.[12] Increasingly, the trend is moving toward incorporating more technology into career development programs through the use of online career centers and computer labs for individualized, self-paced, self-scheduled training.[13]

Employers often provide mentoring programs to assist employees, especially people of color and women, prepare for career opportunities and advancement. Employees are paired with experienced members of the organization to provide professional and personal support, teach the "ropes" of the organization, increase understanding of the organizational climate and politics, and coach toward professional success. Mentoring provides insight into the internal functioning of the organization in areas that may not be known or accessible to groups that have been excluded in the past. Many of these are formal mentoring programs that are developed and implemented by the human resource department. Mentors often receive training regarding the role of mentors and the best approaches to achieve positive mentoring outcomes.

THE GRAYING WORKFORCE

Demographic trends indicate that labor force participation rates of older workers will likely rise in the years ahead.[14] Many baby boomers will work into their seventies and eighties. Longer-term employment is likely to be strongest among the best-educated employees of the baby-boom generation. "Even at age 65 and older, nearly 18.6 percent of college graduates remained in the labor force whereas only 8.1 percent of those without high school diplomas did."[15] Since there are fewer younger workers available to replace baby boomers and increasing needs for highly skilled and educated employees, employers will need to find ways to induce older workers to remain in the workforce longer.[16] These experienced and educated workers can serve as mentors and trainers for new entrants and less experienced employees.

Human resource and department managers can take several steps to ensure that the contributions and the needs of older workers are not ignored.

- Make alternative work schedules available so employees can take care of sick spouses, go back to school, or slow down.
- Offer complete retirement planning seminars and education.

- Provide suitable training and retraining for all staff, especially in the area of technology.
- Work with senior job training programs at local colleges.
- Provide employees with elder care resource and referral help.
- Educate managers and staff on age discrimination.
- Actively recruit older workers for positions.[17]

ASSESSMENT OF TRAINING NEEDS

Now more than ever, public sector organizations must prepare their workforce for the rapid changes in skills, technology, and expertise. Human resource and department managers share the responsibility to assure that their employees develop and maintain state-of-the-art skills and competencies. This requires frequent agencywide assessment to obtain feedback from employees and managers about their changing training and development needs. In today's participatory environment, workers value self-determination and seek opportunities to provide input into matters that directly impact their lives. Assessment surveys, focus groups, and interviews help human resource professionals serve the needs of and provide education and training for an ever changing workforce.

WORK-LIFE PROGRAMS

Twenty-first-century workers bring a new set of expectations and challenges to the workplace. They are working mothers, sandwich generation baby boomers (caring for their children and aging parents at the same time), generation Y and Xers, dual-career spouses, retired part-time or second-career employees, and workers who bring diverse cultures, religions, customs, and preferences. Given the employer's compelling need to attract and retain talented workers, the workplace is being restructured to meet the expectations and needs of this diverse array of employees.

BENEFIT PROGRAMS

The requirements of this new environment have influenced employers to offer work-life programs and benefits that support employees more comprehensively. Although many organizations with work-life programs offer these benefits as across-the-board entitlements, a survey of work-life programs reported that 18 percent (226) of organizations that responded use work-life benefits as rewards for high performers.[18] Other survey respondents indicated that they were considering linking work-life benefits to performance in the future. This inclination suggests that the trend toward performance-linked work-life benefits will gain popularity among employers. According to the survey, benefits that are most often linked to performance include flexible work arrangements (141), tuition reimbursement (101) and paid time off (40).[19] Other benefits that are frequently provided in work-life programs include on-site child care, elder care, wellness/fitness programs, financial planning, legal services, sick and backup child care and child-care referral, casual dress, and time-saving convenience services.[20]

ENABLING TECHNOLOGIES

The growing trend toward teleworking or telecommuting is providing another major work-life linkage for new era workers. Telecommuting or teleworking is defined as "any form of substitution of information technologies (such as telecommunications and/or computers) for normal work-related travel; moving the work to the workers instead of moving the workers to work."[21] Niles, Estes, and Jonas add that teleworking means working remotely from one's colleagues, but being connected to them through telecommunications.[22] They report that "the number of telecommuters working during normal daytime business hours as of 1998 is 15.7 million, which amounts to about 8 percent of the U.S. population age 18 and older."[23] These technologies are especially advantageous to workers who are responsible for parenting and elder care and workers with disabilities.[24]

The *when* and *where* of office work is changing considerably. Sutherland calls the new alternatives for office location "officing."[25] Alternative types of officing in addition to home-based offices include telework centers (multi-company remote offices), satellite offices (single company remote offices), nonterritorial offices (offices not permanently assigned), shared-space hoteling (office space assigned day by day), guesting (office space assigned to one person but used by another temporarily), facilities exchange (offices of one organization used by another), activity settings (special activity space), team suites or teaming space (office space assigned to teams), and watering hole (office space for casual socializing).[26] The selection of an alternative office location depends on the type of work to be accomplished, the need and frequency of required contact with other employees, and the mutual needs of employers and workers. These alternative locations can also facilitate the delivery of training programs and completion of work by welfare-to-work and other inner-city employees who may have difficulty obtaining transportation to suburban locations and obtaining full-time child or elder care.[27]

The benefits of telecommuting programs to employees and managers are substantial.

EMPLOYER BENEFITS

- Increased productivity, stimulated by lower absenteeism, higher employee concentration on work, fewer distractions
- Less travel time, and better use of employees' peak efficiency times
- Decreased turnover because employee morale is higher and work options, such as job or office sharing, become possible once long commutes are eliminated

- Hiring incentive for new employees to join the organization
- An opportunity to tap new labor pools such as parents with young children, persons with disabilities, and others
- Lower overhead because of the lower cost of suburban space and parking

EMPLOYEE BENEFITS
- Financial savings on parking fees, fuel, car maintenance, insurance, and even the need for a second car
- A large reduction in stress
- More time for families and opportunities for community participation
- Fewer distractions on the job, greater work autonomy, and more relaxed work environment
- Time and money saved by not commuting to work [28]

Telecommuting and assistive technologies are increasingly opening up the workplace to employees with disabilities. Assistive technologies include devices such as character readers, voice-recognition devices, and "smart" prostheses. These advances help to increase the available pool of qualified workers and enhance the development of human capital.

Along with the benefits, teleworking presents certain challenges for managers and workers. Managers often express concern that teleworking may increase opportunities for abuse of flexible work hours and thereby reduce productivity. Employees worry that managers may feel justified in assigning additional work, which encroaches on family time or results in overtime hours without appropriate compensation.

This form of work is not suitable for some employees. The telecommuting training program for the Washington State Office of Energy provides a definition for good candidates.

- Self-motivated and responsible
- Results-oriented
- Can work independently
- Familiar and comfortable with their job
- Know all organizational procedures
- Successful in current position
- Effective communicator
- Adaptable
- Committed to telecommuting [29]

In addition to evaluating the suitability of employees for telecommuting, implementation of this form of work raises several other critical issues, including measurement of productivity improvement, changes in employee's overtime, and legal issues including workers' compensation, laws, IRS home-office deductions issues, and employee versus independent contractor status, among others.[30] Consequently, it is essential that human resource managers develop telecommuting training programs along with sound policies and procedures that specify expectations and requirements for managers and employees. Professional organizations such as IPMA and SHRM provide sample policies for public and private organizations as well as provide access to resource links, surveys, and reports on telecommuting.

WORK TEAMS AND DIVERSITY[31]

The focus on diversity in organizations has gained prominence simultaneously with the movement toward team structures in the workplace. The concurrent emergence of these two events provides a prime opportunity for organizations to merge the strengths of diversity with the collaborative vitality of self-directed work teams (SDWTs).

What the initiatives to incorporate diversity and SDWTs have in common is their potential to enhance the quality of performance and innovation by focusing the unique contributions of diverse team members toward a *"common goal or purpose."* SDWTs may provide one of the most natural means for incorporating and promoting diversity in twenty-first-century organizations. Successful collaboration and achievement in these diverse teams require recognizing and developing several mutually dependent factors.

- Sustaining the group's focus on its common goal or purpose
- Having diverse participants provide "group valued" contributions
- Establishing an equitable division of workload
- Agreeing on equitable contributions by team members
- Developing and supporting members as effective leaders and followers
- Encouraging open-mindedness among team members
- Spending focused time together (both work and social time)
- Listening with respect to team members and communicating for the purpose of gaining understanding

AUTONOMY AND EMPOWERMENT

When properly implemented, SDWTs empower employees to assume many of the traditional manager's responsibilities.[32] Team members are jointly responsible for whole work processes, with each individual typically cross-trained to perform multiple tasks.[33] The functioning of SDWTs is based on shared authority, flexible and shared tasks, information sharing, participative decision making, and interdependence.

Self-directed work teams can serve as rewarding and motivating forces for employees who value autonomy and innovation. As Kimball Fisher foretold, "Competitive advantage comes from fully utilizing the *discretionary effort* of the work force, not from buying the latest gadget or using the latest management fad."[34] Though Gibson and Kirkman caution that teams are not the solution for every organization,[35] by giving workers more autonomy and empowering them to accomplish the organization's goals, their workers' energy and talents can be used to get the job done rather than wasted battling over issues of authority.

Empowering workers does not mean that managers have no role. Managers' roles in SDWT structures are recast as coaches, mentors, capacity builders, and securers of resources. To be properly empowered, workers must have access to accurate information; they must have adequate resources and the necessary authority to plan, administer, and implement work activities. This is a far cry from the traditional work system in which managers plan and administer while workers only execute orders.

STRATEGIC HUMAN RESOURCE INITIATIVES FOR DIVERSE SDWTS

The creation and implementation of diverse self-directed work teams must be identified as strategic factors in order for the organization to achieve viability in the future. Structuring diverse SDWTs begins with a process in which human resource managers, department heads, and employees jointly identify specific team projects, goals, and tasks that emerge from the organization's strategic plan. Team members should be selected based on their diverse expertise, experience, capabilities, and backgrounds, including varied gender and ethnic perspectives.

Planning sessions should focus on

- development of appropriate methods for assessing the teams' functioning and outcomes as well as approaches for evaluation of the performance and contributions of individual members;
- creation of a process to assess the team's progress toward its goals and establishment of supporting reward systems;
- identification of the team's work processes, location, and structure; and
- schedule for focused time together (on-site or via telecommunications) to engage in idea generation, problem solving, communication, and collegial interaction.

Human resource managers serve as internal consultants to executive leaders, department managers, and team members to support the transition to SDWTs. This transition requires changing employee reward systems, methods of classification and pay, performance appraisal, work schedules, work locations, and so forth. SDWTs shift the focus of human resource and department managers from solely individual accomplishments to team *and* individual achievements and rewards. When employees work in teams, classification and pay systems require flexible approaches, such as broadbanding. Different forms of performance assessment, for instance 360-degree evaluations or performance-planning appraisal systems, have to accompany changes in work functions and accountability. Effective reward systems should be developed to provide incentives for employees to work as a team while encouraging strong individual contributions. One public sector agency awards bonus pay for high individual achievement and increases the bonus substantially if the whole team's productivity exceeds performance standards. In order to support the new processes inherent in diverse SDWTs, an accompanying training program would include, at minimum, components pertaining to

- planning projects and setting goals;
- making transition from individual to team work;
- aligning personal and organizational goals;
- including cultural, racial, gender, and individual elements of inter-action in a diverse work setting;
- utilizing diversity to enhance team performance and outcomes;
- fostering credibility and self-management;
- serving as an effective leader and follower in SDWTs;
- developing communication competency, including cross-cultural com-munications, disagreeing agreeably, and active listening; and
- cultivating productive work processes in teams.

MANAGEMENT FOR THE NEW MILLENNIUM

Managing the type of diversity described above requires creative manage-ment approaches and innovative strategies for problem solving. The artificial dichotomy of the employee versus the total person has limited managers' ca-pacity to be caring and compassionate, to reach goals, and to understand what employees need to perform at their peak. Since traditional management phi-losophy advocated separation of the employee from the total person, man-agers were led to believe that such separation was not only possible but also necessary for sound practice. Workers were expected to leave their personal life challenges, issues, and aspirations at the front door of the organization. This dichotomy was probably always unrealistic, but in today's society it works against new management philosophies and the employee's desire to have meaningful, committed work and a balanced and caring personal life. The traditional way of managing defines success and distributes rewards based on total dedication to organizational needs and goals, often to the exclu-sion of employees' needs and goals. In practical terms, this means that those who live almost entirely for the organization reap the greatest rewards.

PERSON-CENTERED MANAGEMENT

Person-Centered Management (PCM) [36] is an approach that focuses on the em-ployee as a complex, multifaceted individual whose functioning in the work-place is not isolated from his or her functioning as a total person. Table 8-1 depicts PCM's general characteristics, employee responsibilities, mutual expectations of employees and managers, and responsibilities of human resource managers. The remainder of this chapter explains the components outlined in Table 8-1.

GENERAL CHARACTERISTICS

A good employee-manager relationship using the PCM model incorporates mutual trust, respect, and bona fide concern for each person's welfare. This new era approach starts with the premise that an employee-manager relationship is in fact a professional and personal partnership. It has a unique combination of characteristics that incorporate work, collegiality, or mentoring, and often friendship.

Like any other partnership, PCM requires considerable work by both parties and there is no guarantee that they will remain mutually compatible for the duration of their work life together. However, this approach adds a dimension of genuine human caring, a sense of obligation approaching covenant proportions, and authentic bonding that has not been explicitly espoused in previous management literature.

PCM relies heavily on the concept of authentic employee "empowerment." Yeatts and Hyten point out that managers can empower members of a team by "turning over power, information, knowledge, skills and decision; being a teacher and counselor; being people-oriented and a facilitator rather than a decision maker; removing environmental barriers that hinder teams; being a motivator; and promoting teamwork."[37]

If we examine innovative, high-performing public and private organizations, we will find many of these managers practicing PCM. That is, the emphasis is placed on caring about individual employees, recognizing their stake in the organization, and fully utilizing their motivation, capacity, and ingenuity as the foundation for achieving success.

PCM also requires that managers have considerable knowledge of themselves and employees. Managers need to know the employees' work and personal abilities, strengths, and problem areas, so that they can help employees use their knowledge, skills, and abilities to achieve success. Managers should enhance their own personal capabilities and identify areas that need improvement to enhance their abilities to respond effectively.

MANAGERS' ROLES

PCM changes the roles of managers and their interactions with employees. Employees at the work site and those involved in telecommuting require managers who are flexible, trusting, results-oriented, and able to rely on the capabilities and expertise of the worker. In addition to the complexity of their jobs, employees are dealing with problems as diverse as divorce, stress, child care, elder care, and addictions. More than ever, effective managers must be prepared to handle the impact of these issues in the workplace.

TABLE 8-1	COMPONENTS OF PERSON-CENTERED MANAGEMENT (PCM)

General Characteristics

■ Total-person focus — regards employee as a whole person with multiple roles, capabilities, and needs
■ Views management as a function involving an employee-manager partnership
■ Adds human caring as a component of management
■ Requires authentic empowerment of the employee
■ Requires multiple human responses
■ Requires manager's knowledge of himself/herself and the employee (including manager's and employee's strengths and weaknesses)

Managers' Roles

■ Leader
■ Project director
■ Coach
■ Delegator
■ Facilitator
■ Diagnostician (human and organizational problems)
■ Resource person
■ Colleague/mentor (often includes friendship)
■ Communicator
■ Influencer

Employee Responsibilities

■ Self-direction
■ Personal accountability
■ Personal maturity
■ Focus on common goals
■ Cooperation
■ Information gathering, analysis, and sharing findings or results
■ Independent and group contributions
■ Problem solving related to task/goals

(continued)

Managers in this environment must be project directors, coaches, delegators, facilitators, colleagues/mentors (often includes friendship) and diagnosticians of human and organizational problems who can locate and effectively utilize resources to support employees. These managers need to know how to ask questions, guide a group to consensus, and use that information to demonstrate the need for action.[38] No longer can managers rely solely on traditional factors such as power, authority, and control to accomplish the work.

The key is to cultivate a work climate that allows employees to acquire power, authority, and control over their own jobs. This does not mean that managers have abdicated their responsibility because the goals of managers and workers are closely aligned. In traditional management, one might have referred to this situation as delegation of authority, but in PCM environments, "delegation" is too narrow. PCM is much closer to a mutual form of empowerment.

TABLE 8-1	CONTINUED

Mutual Expectations of Managers and Employees

Job Expectations
- Mutual understanding of work to be accomplished
- Clear work expectations
- Job satisfaction
- Input/involvement in one's own work and in the goals of the unit
- Goal/task completion

Personal Expectations
- Concern for personal well-being
- Recognition of and help with personal concerns that affect job performance
- Fair treatment
- Recognition of individuality
- Respect as a thinking, feeling human being
- Trust
- Mature/adult treatment

Human Resource Manager's Responsibilities

- Create a climate of service and care
- Generate human resource visions, missions, and goals in alignment with the larger organization
- Develop cutting-edge human resource programs and practices
- Create person-centered programs and approaches
- Build capacity among employees and managers to implement person-centered practices
- Develop "core competencies" in human resource management

EMPLOYEE RESPONSIBILITIES

With empowerment come new responsibilities for employees. The strength of the current trends in reorganization has been "the opportunity for all employees to develop the skills and perspectives to take care of themselves, increase their self-esteem, and move beyond the constraints of a codependent organizational relationship."[39] Liberated from the constraints of the paternalistic model, individuals today can leverage change far more effectively than most institutions.

This level of individual responsibility requires self-direction, personal accountability, and maturity. This means that employees have to demonstrate commitment to common goals. In describing the four dimensions of an empowering organization, Lin found that empowered employees feel they have a stake in the goals of their organization.[40] They are characteristically intimately involved in setting these goals and being responsible for the results. They are, furthermore, forced to continuously learn—a feat enabled by the same technology enabling the teleworker described above—in order to "maintain their own credibility."[41]

This focus on individual responsibility does not mean isolation. On the contrary, this environment requires commitment and cooperation with the managers and project team members. Employees are responsible to the team or work unit and themselves for information gathering, analysis, and sharing findings or results. Individual responsibility and group responsibility are not separate concepts, but are overlapping constructs. Employees have responsibilities to the community of coworkers just as the community has obligations to the individuals that constitute it.

When this responsibility is not met, the community (and hence the organization) suffers. In PCM, it does not take a manager or performance evaluation to point out that an individual is not producing his/her share. Rather, the community members will point out the individual's variance from social norms and attempt to facilitate change. The social pressure of not living up to group expectations may be stronger than any performance improvement initiated by managers.

MUTUAL EXPECTATIONS OF MANAGERS AND EMPLOYEES

PCM requires a set of explicit, mutually understood job and personal expectations. Job expectations include issues such as mutual understanding of work to be accomplished and clear performance expectations; input into one's own work and in the goals of the unit; and goal attainment. Personal expectations encompass concern for personal well-being, recognition of and help with personal concerns that affect job performance, fair treatment, recognition of individuality, respect as a thinking, feeling human being, trust, and mature/adult treatment. These factors are discussed during exchanges in which employees and managers work together and understand each other as unique individuals.

Although these job and personal expectations are not totally new in the work environment, they have acquired a new priority and level of importance for organizational success. Attainment of organizational goals is dependent on the abilities of both managers and employees to function successfully. These changes in roles and priorities succeed best in organizations that initiate and sustain PCM practices throughout their structures.

RESPONSIBILITIES OF HUMAN RESOURCE MANAGERS

PCM provides a framework for imaginative human resource management in the new era. The human resource department can lead the way to creating a climate of service and care. This innovation requires openness to finding viable alternatives and the shedding of rule-bound approaches to complex issues.

Progressive personnel managers generate human resource visions, missions, and goals in alignment with the organization and its changing external environment. They develop cutting-edge human resource programs and practices. These managers provide development and training programs to build capacity for sustaining person-centered practices. Significantly, human resource professionals develop their own "core competencies" through specialized training programs such as those offered through IPMA and SHRM. These competencies include the ability to

- understand the public service environment;
- be innovative and create a risk-taking environment;
- use and understand systems thinking;
- think strategically and creatively;
- design and implement processes of change;
- use consensus and coalition-building skills;
- build trusting relationships;
- demonstrate customer service orientation;
- understand, value, and promote diversity;
- understand team behavior; and
- practice and promote integrity and ethical behavior.[42]

PCM is more than a collection of techniques and strategies. It is a philosophy and way of life in organizations. It is time for human resource and department managers to connect the work and lives of public sector employees, to view employees as partners in the pursuit of common goals, and to promote relationships based on trust and care. These are essential elements for meeting the challenges of the new millennium. Department and human resource managers share the responsibility for creating this enlightened future.

NOTES

1. U.S. Department of Labor, *Futurework: Trends and Challenges for Work in the Twenty-first Century—Executive Summary*, in Department of Labor [database online] (Washington, DC: Department of Labor, September 1999 [cited 15 March 2000]), available from http://www.dol.gov.

2. Ibid.

3. Richard W. Judy and Carol D'Amico, "Workforce 2020—Executive Summary," in Hudson Institute [database online] (Indianapolis, IN: Hudson Institute, 1997 [cited 19 March 2000]), access from http://www.hudson.org.

4. Ibid.

5. Richard W. Judy, "Skills for Workforce Growth: 1994–2005: Will There Really Be a Skills Gap?" in Hudson Institute [database online] (Indianapolis, IN: Hudson Institute, 1997 [cited 19 March 2000]), access from http://www.hudson.org.

6. Maureen Smith, "Providing Individuals with Ongoing Skills Development," in IPMA [database online] (Alexandria, VA: IPMA [cited 19 March 2000]), member-restricted access from http://www.ipma-hr.org.

7. Ibid.

8. "The Workforce Investment Partnership Act," SHRM [database online] (Alexandria, VA: SHRM [cited 19 March 2000]), member-restricted access from http://www.shrm.org.

9. Ibid.

10. Maureen Smith, "Implementing Literacy Initiatives in the Workplace," in IPMA [database online] (Alexandria, VA: IPMA [cited 19 March 2000]), member-restricted access from http://www.ipma-hr.org.

11. Ibid.

12. Jane Gold, "Career Development Programs (Part II)," in IPMA [database online] (Alexandria, VA: IPMA, 1997 [cited 15 March 2000]), member-restricted access from http://www.ipma-hr.org.

13. Ibid.

14. Richard W. Judy, "Why More Older Americans Will Be Working in the Early Twenty-first Century" in Hudson Institute [database online] (Indianapolis, IN: Hudson Institute, 1996 [cited 19 March 2000]), access from http://www.hudson.org.

15. Ibid.

16. Ibid.

17. "Graying America's Impact on HR," in IPMA [database online] (Alexandria, VA: IPMA [cited 19 March 2000]), member-restricted access from http://www.ipma-hr.org.

18. Segal Company and American Compensation Association (ACA), "1999 Survey of Performance-Based Work/Life Program," *IPMA News*, January 2000, 19–20.

19. Ibid.

20. Ibid.

21. "What Is Teleworking/Telecommuting?" in IPMA [database online] (Alexandria, VA: IPMA [cited 15 March 2000]), member-restricted access from http://www.ipma-hr.org.

22. John S. Niles, Barbara Estes, and Donald Jonas, "Integrating Telework, Flextime, and Officing for Work Force 2020," in Hudson Institute [database online] (Indianapolis, IN: Hudson Institute, 1998 [cited 19 March 2000]), access from http://www.hudson.org.

23. Ibid.

24. U.S. Department of Labor, *Futurework.*

25. Niles, Estes, and Jonas, "Telework, Flextime, and Officing."

26. Ibid.

27. Ibid.

28. "What Is Teleworking/Telecommuting?"

29. Niles, Estes, and Jonas, "Telework, Flextime, and Officing."

30. Ibid.

31. Much of the information in this section is taken from Hickman and Creighton-Zollar, "Diverse Self-directed Work Teams," 187–200.

32. Ibid., 187.

33. Ibid.

34. Kimball Fisher, *Leading Self-Directed Work Teams: A Guide to Developing New Team Leadership Skills* (New York: McGraw-Hill, 1993), 13.

35. Cristina B. Gibson and Bradley L. Kirkman, " Our Past, Present, and Future in Teams: The Role of Human Resource Professionals in Managing Team Performance," in *Evolving Practices in Human Resource Management*, eds. Allen Kraut and Abraham Korman (San Francisco: Jossey-Bass, 1999), 94.

36. The coauthor conceptualized this term and its characteristics in the late 1980s. It was presented originally in Gill D. Robinson, "Person-Centered Management," *Black Women of Achievement Magazine* (NAACP Legal Defense Fund, Inc.) 1 (1) (1988). The coauthor later conducted a workshop titled "Person-Centered Management and the Employee Discipline Process" for the Management Employees Association, Harbor-UCLA in 1988, using an early version of PCM. James E. Tingstad also used the term PCM in "Why Do Technical Managers Ignore the Data?" *Research-Technology Management* 35 (January/February 1992): 8–9. More recently, a similar and expanded concept was detailed in Jeanne M. Plas, *Person-Centered Leadership: An American Approach to Participatory Management* (Thousand Oaks, CA: Sage, 1996).

37. Dale E. Yeatts and Cloyd Hyten, *High-Performing Self-Managed Work Teams: A Comparison of Theory to Practice* (Thousand Oaks, CA: Sage, 1998), 193.

38. Ibid., 190–196.

39. David M. Noer, "Helping Organizations Change: Coping with Downsizing, Mergers, Reengineering, and Reorganizations," in *Evolving Practices in Human Resource Management*, eds. Allen Kraut and Abraham Korman (San Francisco: Jossey-Bass, 1999), 294.

40. Carol Yeh-Yun Lin, "The Essence of Empowerment: A Conceptual Model and a Case Illustration," *Journal of Applied Management Studies* 7 (2): 224 (1998).

41. Ibid.

42. Partial list of core competencies taken from "Agency Issues, Volume 23, Number 9," in IPMA [database online] (Alexandria, VA: IPMA, 19 May 1997 [cited 19 March 2000]), member-restricted access restricted from http://www.ipma-hr.org.

PREEMPLOYMENT INQUIRY GUIDELINES (FROM SIMMONS, *EMPLOYMENT DISCRIMINATION*, 575–576)

Acceptable	Subject	Unacceptable
Name "Have you ever used another name?" /or/ "Is any additional information relative to change of name, use of an assumed name, or nickname necessary to enable a check on your work and education record? If yes, please explain."	Name	Maiden name
Place of residence	Residence	"Do you own or rent your home?"
Statement that hire is subject to verification that applicant meets legal age requirements "If hired, can you show proof of age?" "Are you over eighteen years of age?" "If under eighteen, can you, after employment, submit a work permit?"	Age	Age Birth date Dates of attendance or completion of elementary or high school Questions which tend to identify applicants over age forty
"Can you, after employment, submit verification of your legal right to work in the United States?" /or/ Statement that such proof may be required after a decision is made to hire the candidate	Birthplace, citizenship	Birthplace of applicant, applicant's parents, spouse, or other relatives "Are you a U.S. citizen?" /or/ Citizenship of applicant, applicant's parents, spouse, or other relatives Requirements that applicant produce naturalization, first papers, or alien card *prior to a decision to hire*

Acceptable	Subject	Unacceptable
Language applicant reads, speaks, or writes, if use of a language other than English is relevant to the job for which applicant is applying	National origin	Requirements that applicant produce naturalization, first papers, or alien card *prior to a decision to hire* Questions about nationality, lineage, ancestry, national origin, descent, or parentage of applicant, applicant's parents, or spouse "What is your mother tongue?" /or/ Language commonly used by applicant How applicant acquired ability to read, write, or speak a foreign language
Name and address of parent or guardian if applicant is a minor Statement of company policy regarding work assignment of employees who are related	Sex, marital status, family	Questions which indicate applicant's sex Questions which indicate applicant's marital status Number and/or ages of children or dependents Provisions for child care Questions regarding pregnancy, childbearing, or birth control Name and address of relative, spouse, or children of adult applicant "With whom do you reside?" /or/ "Do you live with your parents?"
	Race, color	Questions about applicant's race or color Questions regarding applicant's complexion or color of skin, eyes, hair
	Credit report	Any report which would indicate information which is otherwise illegal to ask, e.g., marital status, age, residency, etc.
Statement that a photograph may be required after employment	Physical description, photograph	Questions about applicant's height and weight Require applicant to affix a photograph to application Require a photograph after interview but before employment Videotaping interviews

Acceptable	Subject	Unacceptable
Statement by employer that offer may be made contingent on applicant passing a job-related physical examination "Can you perform (specific task)?"	Physical or mental disability	Questions regarding applicant's general medical condition, state of health, or illnesses Questions regarding receipt of worker's compensation "Do you have any physical or mental disabilities or handicaps?"
Statement by employer of regular days, hours, or shifts to be worked	Religion	Questions regarding applicant's religion Religious days observed /or/ "Does your religion prevent you from working weekends or holidays?"
Job-related questions about *convictions*, except those convictions which have been sealed, expunged, or statutorily eradicated	Arrest, criminal record	Arrest record /or/ "Have you ever been arrested?" (This is a violation of California Labor Code Section 432.7, which is enforced by the labor commissioner.)
Questions regarding relevant skills acquired during applicant's U.S. military service	Military service	General questions regarding military service such as dates and type of discharge Questions regarding service in a foreign military
"Please list job-related organizations, clubs, professional societies, or other associations to which you belong — you may omit those which indicate your race, religious creed, color, disability, marital status, national origin, ancestry, sex, or age."	Organizations, activities	"List all organizations, clubs, societies, and lodges to which you belong."
"By whom were you referred for a position here?" Names of persons willing to provide professional and/or character references for applicant	References	Questions of applicant's former employers or acquaintances which elicit information specifying the applicant's race, color, religious creed, national origin, ancestry, physical or mental disability, medical condition, marital status, age, or sex.
Name and address of person to be notified in case of accident or emergency	Notice in case of emergency	Name, address, and relationship of relative to be notified in case of accident or emergency

SAMPLE GUIDELINES FOR POSITION CLASSIFICATION

- Sample Position Description Form
- Sample Guidelines for Writing a Position Description in Accordance with Allocation Factors

ALLOCATION FACTORS

1. NATURE AND VARIETY OF WORK
Describe the various kinds of work involved in this position. Provide a *complete* description of duties. Most positions have at least seven to ten duties or more. Indicate how frequently these duties are performed.

2. TYPE OF GUIDELINES AVAILABLE
Describe the written and/or oral instructions or assistance available to help in understanding and performing job duties.

3. TYPE OF SUPERVISION RECEIVED
- Close supervision—supervisor reviews most tasks
- Intermediate supervision—supervisor reviews final product
- General supervision—very broad; supervisor only discusses unusual situations

4. DECISION-MAKING AUTHORITY
- Limited—employee makes very few decisions
- Intermediate—employee acts after consulting supervisor
- Considerable—employee makes most decisions independently

5. ORIGINALITY/CREATIVITY
Employee develops new programs, methods, procedures, and/or formats as a part of the job. Describe examples.

6. PERSON-TO-PERSON CONTACT

Describe the amount of personal contact (daily, weekly, monthly, annually, not applicable) required to perform the job, and describe the purpose of the contact with

- the public;
- top/executive managers;
- managers/supervisors within organization;
- other employees in own office;
- employees in other offices; or
- managers/supervisors in other organizations.

7. SUPERVISION OVER OTHERS

In employee's role as supervisor, how many employees does he or she supervise? Does he or she

- hire staff or give effective recommendation for hiring;
- train staff;
- assign work;
- evaluate performance;
- recommend disciplinary action;
- recommend pay increases?

8. QUALIFICATION REQUIREMENTS (ACTUAL REQUIREMENTS FOR JOB PERFORMANCE)

- Education requirements
- Knowledge, skills, and abilities required
- Years of experience in (name field or area of expertise)
- Licenses required
- Other qualifications required

POSITION DESCRIPTION

Name _____ Date _____

Position Title _____ Dept./Div. _____

INSTRUCTIONS: Complete each of the sections as fully and accurately as possible. Use the Guidelines for Writing a Position Description to assist in the development of the description.

Often	Occasionally	Seldom	**DESCRIPTION OF DUTIES**
			Describe in clear and specific terms the duties and responsibilities of this position and the percentage of overall time spent performing each. Please use additional sheets if necessary.

2. Guidelines Available

3. Type of Supervision Received

4. Decision-Making Authority

5. Originality/Creativity

6. Person-to-Person Contact

SUPERVISORY RESPONSIBILITIES

If this is a supervisory position, list the names and titles of those directly and indirectly supervised. (The definition of supervision for this purpose is the responsibility for hiring, training, assigning work, and recommending merit and disciplinary action.) Further, describe your responsibilities and duties with regard to these employees.

QUALIFICATION REQUIREMENTS

Identify the actual (not necessarily the current) requirements for job performance, including education; knowledge and abilities required (very important); years of experience in a specific area, skill, or field; licenses required, if any; and any other requirements

IPMA STATEMENT OF PRINCIPLES AND VALUES

As a member of the International Personnel Management Association, I pledge:

- To support the Association's goals and objectives for developing the human resource management professional and the public's understanding of the role of human resource management;

- To maintain the highest standard of professional competence and of professional and personal conduct;

- To respect the dignity of all individuals, and to protect people's rights to fair and equitable treatment in all aspects of employment without regard to race, sex, religion, age, national origin, disability, or any other non-merit or non-job-related factor, and to promote affirmative action;

- To support my employer's legitimate efforts for a qualified and productive workforce to accomplish my employer's mission;

- To emphasize the importance of addressing the impact of managers' plans and decisions on people;

- To support, mentor and counsel individuals pursuing a career in human resource management;

- To treat as privileged and confidential information accepted in trust;

- To uphold all federal, state and local laws, ordinances and regulations, and endeavor to instill in the public a sense of confidence and trust about the conduct and actions of my employer and myself;

- To avoid a conflict of interest; and

- To not compromise, for personal gain or benefit or special privilege, my integrity or that of my employer.

This Code of Professional Principles and Statement of Values for the International Personnel Management Association was adopted as revised by the Executive Council on Saturday, October 5, 1991.

BIBLIOGRAPHY

"Agency Issues." In IPMA archives [database online]. Alexandria, VA: IPMA, May 1997—[cited 9 March 2000]. Access restricted to members at http://www.ipma-hr.org.

"An Employers Guide to an Anti-Sexual Harassment Plan." In IPMA archives [database online]. Alexandria, VA: IPMA, 1997—[cited 8 March 2000]. Access restricted to members at http://www.ipma-hr.org.

A Major Malfunction: The Story Behind the Space Shuttle Challenger Disaster. Mark Maier, dir. Binghamton, NY: Research Foundation of the State University, 1992.

Ban, Carolyn, and Norma Riccucci, eds. *Public Personnel Management: Current Concerns, Future Challenges.* New York: Longman, 1997.

"Broadbanding in the Public Sector." *Broadbanding: Volume III.* In IPMA archives [database online]. Alexandria, VA: IPMA, May 1997—[cited 8 March 2000]. Access restricted to members at http://www.ipma-hr.org.

Cardy, Robert L. "Performance Appraisal in a Quality Context: A New Look at an Old Problem." In *Performance Appraisal: State of the Art in Practice,* edited by James W. Smither. San Francisco: Jossey-Bass, 1998.

Chambers, Tamu, and Norma M. Riccucci. "Models of Excellence in Workplace Diversity." In *Public Personnel Management: Current Concerns, Future Challenges,* edited by Carolyn Ban and Norma M. Riccucci, 73–90. New York: Longman, 1997.

"Dealing with Workplace Violence: A Guide for Agency Planners—Part I, Section 1." Accessed 8 March 2000 from http://www.opm.gov.workplac/handbook/pl-s3.htm.

Digh, Patricia. "In and Out of the Corporate Closet." In Society for Human Resource Management [database online]. Alexandria, VA: Society for Human Resource Management [cited 19 March 2000]. Member-restricted access from http://www.shrm.org.

Driscoll, Dawn-Marie, W. Michael Hoffman, and Joseph E. Murphy. "Business Ethics and Compliance: What Management Is Doing and Why." *Business and Society Review* (fall 1999): 35–51.

"Employee Recognition & Rewards II." *CPR Series.* In IPMA archives [database online]. Alexandria, VA: IPMA, May 1997—[cited 8 March 2000]. Access restricted to members at http://www.ipma-hr.org.

Farnsworth, E. Allan. *Contracts.* 3d ed. New York: Aspen, 1999.

Fisher, Kimball. *Leading Self-Directed Work Teams.* New York: McGraw-Hill, 1993.

Fox, James, and Charles Klein. "The 360-Degree Evaluation." *Public Management* 78 (November 1996): 20–22.

"Gainsharing." *CPR Series.* In IPMA archives [database online]. Alexandria, VA: IPMA, May 1997—[cited 8 March 2000]. Access restricted to members at http://www.ipma-hr.org.

Gardenswartz, Lee, and Anita Rowe. "Diversity Q&A: How Do I Balance the Rights of All Employees When Accommodating Gays and Lesbians in the Workforce." In Society for Human Resource Management [database online]. Alexandria, VA: Society for Human Resource Management [cited 8 March 2000]. Member-restricted access from http://www.shrm.org.

Gibson, Cristina B., and Bradley L. Kirkman. "Our Past, Present, and Future in Teams: The Role of Human Resource Professionals in Managing Team Performance." In *Evolving Practices in Human Resource Management*, edited by Allen Kraut and Abraham Korman. San Francisco: Jossey-Bass, 1999.

Giddens, Brent M., and Weston A. Edwards. "Communicable Diseases in the Workplace: How to Handle the Risks." In SHRM White Paper [database online]. Alexandria, VA: SHRM, March 1999—[cited 24 March 2000]. Access restricted to members at http://www.shrm.org.

Gold, Jane. "Career Development Programs (Part II)." In IPMA archives [database online]. Alexandria, VA: IPMA, 1997 [cited 15 March 2000]. Access restricted to members at http://www.ipma-hr.org.

"Graying America's Impact on HR." In IPMA archives [database online]. Alexandria, VA: IPMA—[cited 19 March 2000]. Access restricted to members at http://www.ipma-hr.org.

Grote, Dick. *Public Sector Organizations: Today's Innovative Leaders in Performance Management*. In IPMA archives [database online]. Alexandria, VA: IPMA, 1999 [cited 8 March 2000]. Access restricted to members at http://www.ipma-hr.org.

Guy, Mary Ellen. *Ethical Decision Making in Everyday Work Situations*. New York: Quorum Books, 1990.

Hamman, John A., and Uday Desai. "Current Issues in Recruitment and Selection." In *Public Personnel Administration: Problems and Prospects*, edited by Steven W. Hays and Richard C. Kearney, 89–104. Englewood Cliffs, NJ: Prentice Hall, 1995.

Hersey, Paul, Kenneth H. Blanchard, and Dewey E. Johnson. *Management of Organizational Behavior: Utilizing Human Resources*. 7th ed. Upper Saddle River, NJ: Prentice Hall, 1996.

Hickman, Gill R., and Ann Creighton-Zollar. "Diverse Self-Directed Work Teams: Developing Strategic Initiatives for Twenty-first Century Organizations." *Public Personnel Management* 27 (summer 1998): 187–200.

"History of Broadbanding." *Broadbanding: Volume III*. In IPMA archives [database online]. Alexandria, VA: IPMA, May 1997—[cited 8 March 2000]. Access restricted to members at http://www.ipma-hr.org.

HR Explanation and Advice. New York: Research Institute of America Group, 1997.

Judy, Richard W. "Skills for Workforce Growth: 1994–2005: Will There Really Be a Skills Gap?" In Hudson Institute [database online]. Indianapolis, IN: Hudson Institute, 1997 [cited 19 March 2000]. Available from http://www.hudson.org.

———. "Why More Older Americans Will Be Working in the Early Twenty-first Century." In Hudson Institute [database online]. Indianapolis, IN: Hudson Institute, 1996 [cited 19 March 2000]. Available from http://www.hudson.org.

Judy, Richard W., and Carol D'Amico. "Workforce 2020—Executive Summary." In Hudson Institute [database online]. Indianapolis, IN: Hudson Institute, 1997 [cited 19 March 2000]. Available from http://www.hudson.org.

Kearney, Richard C. *Labor Relations in the Public Sector*, 2nd ed. New York: Marcel Dekker, 1992.

Lee, Dalton S. "The Difficulty with Ethics Education in Public Administration." *International Journal of Public Administration* 13 (1 & 2): 181–205 (1990).

Leitner, Peter M., and Ronald J. Stupak. "Ethics, National Security and Bureaucratic Reality: North Knight and Designated Liars." *American Review of Public Administration* 27 (1): 61–75 (1997).

Lewis, Carol W. *The Ethics Challenge in Public Service*. San Francisco: Jossey-Bass, 1991.

Lin, Carol Yeh-Yun. "The Essence of Empowerment: A Conceptual Model and a Case Illustration." *Journal of Applied Management Studies* 7 (2): 223–238 (1998).

Lowry, Phillip E. "A Survey of the Assessment Center Process in the Public Sector." *Public Personnel Management* 25 (summer 1996): 307–321.

Lustig, Joe. "Dating in the Workplace." In IPMA archives [database online]. Alexandria, VA: IPMA [cited 8 March 2000]. Access restricted to members at http://www.ipma-hr.org.

Luthy, John. "New Keys to Employee Performance and Productivity." *Public Management* 80 (March 1998):4–8.

"Make Sure Your Policy's Not a Smoking Gun." In IPMA archives [database online]. Alexandria, VA: IPMA—[cited 8 March 2000]. Access restricted to members at http://www.ipma-hr.org.

National Institute for Occupational Safety and Health. "Violence in the Workplace: Risk Factors and Prevention Strategies. In Current Intelligence Bulletin 57, DHHS (NIOSH) Publication nos. 96–100, 1996. Also available at http://www.cdc.gove/niosh/violhomi.html.

Niles, John S., Barbara Estes, and Donald Jonas. "Integrating Telework, Flextime, and Officing for Work Force 2020." In Hudson Institute [database online]. Indianapolis, IN: Hudson Institute, 1998 [cited 19 March 2000]. Available from http://www.hudson.org.

Noer, David M. "Helping Organizations Change: Coping with Downsizing, Mergers, Reengineering, and Reorganizations." In Evolving Practices in Human Resource Management, edited by Allen Kraut and Abraham Korman. San Francisco: Jossey-Bass, 1999.

O'Neil, Sandra L. "Broadbanding." Society for Human Resource Management [database online]. http://www.shrm.org/docs/whitepapers/wp4.html (2 September 1997).

Park, Hun-Joon. "Can Business Ethics Be Taught? A New Model of Business Ethics Education." Journal of Business Ethics 17 (9/10): 965–977 (1998).

"Pay for Performance: Focus on Organizational and Individual Performance." IPMA CPR Series: Pay for Performance. In IPMA archives [database online]. Alexandria, VA: IPMA, May 1997—[cited 9 March 2000]. Access restricted to members at http://www.ipma-hr.org.

Perry, James L. "Compensation, Merit Pay and Motivation." In Public Personnel Administration: Problems and Prospects, edited by Steven Hays and Richard C. Kearney, 121–132. Englewood Cliffs, NJ: Prentice Hall, 1995.

"Placing Positions into Bands." Broadbanding: Volume III. In IPMA archives [database online]. Alexandria, VA: IPMA, May 1997—[cited 9 March 2000]. Access restricted to members at http://www.ipma-hr.org.

Pynes, Joan E., ed. Human Resources Management for Public and Nonprofit Organizations. San Francisco: Jossey-Bass, 1997.

Riccucci, Norma M. "Will Affirmative Action Survive into the Twenty-first Cen-

tury?" In Public Personnel Management: Current Concerns, Future Challenges, edited by Carolyn Ban and Norma M. Riccucci, 57–72. New York: Longman, 1997.

Robinson, Gill D. "Person-Centered Management." Black Women of Achievement Magazine 1 (1) (1988).

"Sample Policy on AIDS." In SHRM White Paper [database online]. Alexandria, VA: SHRM, July 1999—[cited 24 March 2000]. Access restricted to members at http://www.shrm.org.

Segal Company and American Compensation Association (ACA). "1999 Survey of Performance-Based Work/Life Program. IPMA News. January 19, 2000.

Simmons, Richard. Employment Discrimination and EEO Practice Manual. Van Nuys, CA: Castle, 1996.

Sims, Randi, and Thomas L. Leon. "The Influence of Organizational Expectations on Ethical Decision Making Conflict." The Journal of Business Ethics 23 (2000): 219–228.

Smith, Maureen. "Providing Individuals with Ongoing Skills Development." In IPMA archives [database online]. Alexandria, VA: IPMA, 1997—[cited 19 March 2000]. Access restricted to members at http://www.ipma-hr.org.

———. "Implementing Literacy Initiatives in the Workplace." In IPMA archives [database online]. Alexandria, VA: IPMA, 1997—[cited 19 March 2000]. Access restricted to members at http://www.ipma-hr.org.

Stahl, O. Glenn. Public Personnel Administration. 8th ed. New York: Harper and Row, 1983.

"Strengths and Weaknesses of Broadbanding Systems." Broadbanding: Volume III. In IPMA archives [database online]. Alexandria, VA: IPMA, May 1997—[cited 9 March 2000]. Access restricted to members at http://www.ipma-hr.org.

Tingstad, James E. "Why Do Technical Managers Ignore the Data?" Research Technology Management 35 (1992): 8–9.

Tornow, Walter W., Manuel London, and CCL Associates. "The Challenges and Implications for Maximizing 360-Degree Feedback." In Maximizing the Value of 360-Degree Feedback: A Process for Successful Individual and Organizational Development, 249–258. San Francisco: Jossey-Bass, 1998.

U.S. Department of Labor. *Futurework: Trends and Challenges for Work in the Twenty-first Century—Executive Summary.* In Department of Labor [database online] Washington, DC: Department of Labor, September 1999—[cited 15 March 2000]. Available from http://www.dol.gov.

U.S. Department of Labor, Wage and Hour Division. "Family and Medical Leave Act, as revised 7-1-98." *Code of Federal Regulations,* Title 29, vol. 3, pts. 500–899.

U.S. Equal Employment Opportunity Commission. "Uniform Guidelines on Employee Selection Procedures." *Federal Register* (25 August 1978), vol. 43, pt. 4.

U.S. Equal Employment Opportunity Commission. "Federal Laws Prohibiting Job Discrimination Questions and Answers." [database online]. Washington, DC, 1998—[cited March 2000]. Available at http://www.eeoc.gov/facts.

U.S. Office of Personnel Management. "1938 Advisory Council Report—The Social Security Board's Comments and Recommendations." In Office of Personnel Management [database online]. Washington, DC: Office of Personnel Management—[cited 20 June 2000]. Available from http://www.opm.gov.

"Unleashing the Power of Your Workforce." In IPMA archives [database online]. Alexandria, VA: IPMA, May 1997—[cited 8 March 2000]. Access restricted to members at http://www.ipma-hr.org.

"What is Teleworking/Telecommuting?" In IPMA archives [database online]. Alexandria, VA: IPMA, May 1997—[cited 15 March 2000]. Access restricted to members at http://www.ipma-hr.org.

Winston, Michael G. "Leadership of Renewal: Leadership for the Twenty-first Century." *Business Forum* 22 (winter 1997): 4–7.

"The Workforce Investment Partnership Act." In SHRM [database online]. Alexandria, VA: SHRM, 2 November 1999—[cited 19 March 2000]. Access restricted to members at http://www.shrm.org.

"Workplace Violence Continues to Rise." In HR News Online [database online]. Alexandria, VA: SHRM, 2 November 1999—[cited 13 March 2000]. Access restricted to members at http://www.shrm.org.

Yearta, Shawn K., Sally Maitlis, and Rob B. Briner. "An Exploratory Study of Goal Setting in Theory and Practice: A Motivational Technique That Works?" *Journal of Occupational and Organizational Psychology* 68 (September 1995): 237–252.

Yeatts, Dale E., and Cloyd Hyten. *High-Performing Self-Managed Work Teams: A Comparison of Theory to Practice.* Thousand Oaks, CA: Sage, 1998.

INDEX

CREDITS

Page 40   Illustrations by Frank Paine. Used with permission.

Page 147   "Pre-Employment Inquiry Guidelines" reproduced with permission from *Employment Discrimination and EEO Practice Manual*, 6th ed., Attorney Richard J. Simmons, pp. 575–576. Van Nuys, CA: Castle Publications, Ltd.

Page 155   Reproduced with permission of the International Personnel Management Association (IPMA), Alexandria, VA, www.ipma-hr.org, 703-549-7100.